ANTICHRIST CONNECTION:

COMING FROM THE TRIBE OF DAN

BY

FRANCIS M. RUCHUGO

DORRANCE
PUBLISHING CO
EST. 1920
PITTSBURGH, PENNSYLVANIA 15238

Dorrance Publishing Co
585 Alpha Drive
Suite 103
Pittsburgh, PA 15238
Visit our website at *www.dorrancebookstore.com*

ISBN: 978-1-4809-1861-0
eISBN: 978-1-4809-1838-2

I lovingly dedicate this book to my faithful children, Tiffany, April, Edward and Naomi, whose sincere friendship has refreshed me over the years in a way that words could never express.

I am also grateful to all of them for their continuous encouragement and their untiring effort to see that all I needed in preparation for this book was provided. After my operation of the eyes three years ago, they made sure that I went to church on time and also kept my doctor's appointments on time. While others were in school, Tiffany made sure that all my needs were met including, running errands of all kinds. Thank you, children, for making your daddy proud. Without you nothing would have been possible.

ACKNOWLEDGMENTS

I want to express my gratitude to Deacon Mike Woiwode for his assistance in preparation of this manuscript, and also to those who have been a financial blessing to make it possible.

Last but not least, I want to express my deepest appreciation and gratitude to our church family at St. Leo's Catholic Church, Father Justin Waltz, and others who have been great encouragements as well. Thank you for being with me through blessing and adversity. Your prayers have been heard.

CONTENTS

All scripture references are from the authorized King James
Version of The Bible, printed in the United States of America
for world-wide distribution.

Introduction

Ever since there was war in Heaven in the throne of God against Satan, there have been continuous wars between God's people and those influenced by evil in the last six thousand years. God himself has allowed man to be tempted by Satan, only to prove his sovereignty as the most high God who rules in the kingdom of men. His triumphant ways, in which he overcomes evil and wins victories over Satan is marvelous. Frequently we find that God allows a tempter to try his people for only known given reason by him. A very good example can be seen in the Book of Job, and again in the Book of Matthew Chapter 4:1-11. Over the last six thousand years in history, we have seen similar occurrences of good versus evil and in most cases good prevails over evil. And, in the days of these kings, shall the God of Heaven set up a kingdom, which shall never be destroyed and the kingdom shall not be left to other people but it shall break in pieces and consume all those kingdoms and it shall stand forever. This is the eternal Kingdom of God built on the ruins of the sinful empires of man (Daniel 2:44).

We can see such empires as the flood in Noah's time when man was evil and God destroyed all people during that time except Noah's family. Then several hundred years later, we see King Nimrod, who began to be a mighty hunter before the Lord and the beginning of his kingdom was Babel and Erech and Accad Caineh in the Land of Shimar. This king was organizing people to build a tower of bricks to reach Heaven to the throne of God. And, when God knew what they were doing, he came down and confused their languages and scattered them abroad and they stopped building the tower. One most important lesson to learn there is that when you build with bricks, you go as high as you want. But when you build with stones, you cannot go high because stones are not the same size and shape but bricks are. So the confusing of languages means the scattering of people in different locations where they can invent and discover other means of making a living instead of just making bricks. After that some started forming and growing different crops, others raising animals, others started metal work and producing hunting weapons. Before long, they introduced stock exchange system and set up a market place to sell or exchange their goods. So, they left Nimrod's one-world government system to advance their God-given gifts and talents. This one-world government is now being formed, which will be strong enough in coming years to control the whole world.

Surprisingly, President Obama has been mentioned to become the leader of this body and he is the great, great grandson of King Nimrod. See the descendants of Canaan (Genesis 10:11-20) who went to Egypt and spread to other parts of Africa have a role to play at the end.

Many years have now passed and now we come to another evil affair happening to mankind, the incident of Sodom and Gemorah with the daughters of Lot. The destruction of Sodom and Gemorah because of the evil that took place in the region. Read Genesis 19:1-28. After these things, the children of Israel go to Egypt for 430 years and God heard their cry and was ready to bring them to the Promised Land that he had promised to their fathers. The King of Egypt the Pharaoh refused to let them go, but the hand of the Lord was too strong for Pharaoh. So, God overcame Pharaoh and led the children of Israel across the Red Sea to the Promised Land. Here once again we see the sovereignty of God at work. After they got back to the Promised Land, they faced opposition by existing tribes in various parts of the Land. In the process of all this they were all able to occupy their lots except Dan, who we are going to see again in the story ahead. The children of Israel continued to be dominated by foreign powers for the next several hundred years. Being taken to Babylonian captivity by Nebuchadnezzar the King, then the Medeo-Persia, the Assyrians, the Greeks, and the Romans. Then we saw the defiling and contamination of the Jerusalem temple by Antiochus Eppiphenes, who claimed to be God and judge of the people of God in Israel. Jesus came not too long after this and conquered the Devil and destroyed sin, so that we may obtain salvation through him.

He established his church through his Apostles and promised to come again to take us to our eternal destination where we will reign with him forever and ever. Nevertheless, the Church was allowed to be tested just as the Jews have been tested over the ages. As Christians we have been assured by Christ in Matthew 16:18-19 that the gates of Hell will not prevail against his church. As he has overcome all these trials and tribulations by the devil against his people and his church, let us now move forward with our hearts clean and wait for his second coming. In the upcoming story about who the Antichrist will be and his origin, you will find random repetitions of characters and events. This does not mean that such characters and events are repeated; it means you have to pay attention to them because they emphasize an important point for understanding purposes. (E.g. Behold he shall come like a lion from the swelling of Jordan against the inhabitants of the strong, but I will suddenly make him run away from her. And who is a chosen man that I may appoint over her? For who is like me? And who will appoint me the time? And who is that shepherd that will stand before me? (Jeremiah 49:19)) Now, if you go to Jeremiah 50:44, you will see the same verse repeated, exactly the same way to emphasize the point that God means what He says. Such repetitions will help the reader to understand what the writer is explaining about the character in a given situation. There is a period which is referred to as the silent period or the period between the Testaments which was very critical to Israel as they moved from Old Testament to New Testament. So many changes took place in Palestine, so the Greeks were being overtaken by the Romans after the Punic Wars. In this period also, no prophet was seen in Israel after Malachi until the rising of John the Baptist. The Romans had already taken control of Palestine before the birth of Christ, and it was at this time that the Temple of Jerusalem was dominated by the high priests from the Pharisees group, which is usually from the family of Maccabees who, after the war with the Greeks, appointed themselves high priests.

Around 10-4 B.C. Rome elected Herod of Edom to be governor of Israel, and at that time, Jesus was born. The high priest that came from the family of Maccabees, who later called themselves Pharisees took part in judging Christ and giving him up for Crucifixion. We will see all that in the story. Another thing I would like to say is that this work is not in ascending order because of its nature of searching the scriptures. What I mean by that is that you may see the beginning of the story does not come from Genesis or even Exodus. It may come from the middle of the Bible, or even from the Book of Revelation. However, all these connections will bring us to the point and to the results that we are seeking. If we pay attention to Genesis 49:8-12 and 16-18, and then Revelation 19:11-16 we will be fine in putting all these other pieces together.

CHAPTER ONE:

ADDRESS TO ISRAEL

One Nation, One Lord, and One God

"Hear, O Israel: The Lord our God is one Lord. And thou shall love your God with all thy heart and all thy soul and with all thy might. And these words which I command thee this day shall be in thine heart." (Deut 6:4-6). Here, God is trying to let the children of Israel know that they were also living among other Gods of Canaan such as Baals and should always know who to worship and serve. In Exodus 20:1-6 God reminds the children of Israel again that He is the God that brought them out of the land of Egypt and out of the house of bondage and that they should not love other Gods before him. He is telling them that they should not make graven images to imitate the Gods of Amorites or Phillistines as images of such Gods were common those days. In Verses 4, 5, and 6 God is trying to show them God is invisible and any idol intended to resemble Him would be a sinful representation of Him. He tells them that He is a jealous God, and they should not bow down to worship or serve those other Gods.

Now that God has revealed himself to Moses and to the children of Israel and has commanded them to worship and serve Him alone, as Jesus also reminded the devil in the wilderness that it is written, "Thou shall not tempt the Lord your God and Him only shall you worship and serve." (Matthew 4:1-11) Let us now examine who will listen and obey as we move on with our research for the man of sin.

In the Book of John 1:1, the scripture begins like this, "In the beginning was the word and the word was with God, and the word was God. The same was in the beginning with God. All things were made by Him, and without Him, was not anything made that was made. In Him was life and the life was the light of men. And the light shineth in the darkness, and the darkness comprehended it not." (John 1:1-5) In this scripture, I noticed that there are three who bear witness and these three are equal. Then I remembered back in my high school math class was a section called Geometry. In this Geometry class we learned about equilateral triangles. Triangles with all three sides equal. Then I also realized that this was the Holy Trinity. One day, I was doing my normal reading on the history of the Jew's people. I came across the flag of Israel, which has two equilateral triangles intersecting each other in the center. I stopped and tried to make sense of this mystery. I knew the first triangle was the Holy Trinity, but what was the other triangle? Some people call this the Star of David or the Sceptre, Which will not depart from him." (Genesis 49:10) But what does it mean?

I started thinking about Esau and Jacob in their mother's womb:

> When Rebekkah conceived, the children struggled within her and she said, "If it be so why am I thus?" And she went to enquire of the Lord. And the Lord said unto her, Two nations are in thy womb and two manners of people shall be separated from thy bowels, and the one people shall be stronger than the other people and the elder shall serve the younger. When the days to be delivered were fulfilled, beheld there were twins in her womb. And the first came out red all over like a hairy garment, and they called his name Esau. And after that came his brother out, and his hand took hold on Esau's heel, and his name was called Jacob, and Isaac was threescore years old when she bore them. (Genesis 25:21-26).

Could these two triangles here be two nations? If it is, does it mean that they will crash each other in fighting and wars as they did in their mother's womb? This struggle that started in the womb has gone on through the ages and is still going on. Secondly, I thought about the two covenants in the Book of Galatians:

> Tell me, ye that desires to be under the law, do ye not hear the law? For it is written that Abraham had two sons, the one by a bondmaid, the other by a freewoman. But he who was of bondwoman was born after the flesh, but he who was born

of the freewoman was by promise. Which things are an allegory for these are the two covenants, the one from Mt. Sainai which gendereth to bondage which is *A'gar*. For this *A'gar* is Mt. Sainai in Arabia and answereth to Jerusalem, which now is and is in bondage with her children. Jerusalem, which is above is free, which is the mother of us all.

For it is written, Rejoice, thou barren that bearest not, break forth and cry, thou that traveilest not, for the desolate hath more children than she, who has a husband.

Now we brethren as Isaac was are the children of promise. But, as then he that was born after the flesh persecuted him that was born after the spirit, even so it is now.

Nevertheless, what says the scripture? Cast out the bondwoman and her son for the son of the bondwoman shall not be heir with the son of the freewoman. So then, brethren, we are not children of the bondwoman but of the free (Galatians 4:21-31). Could these double triangles represent the two covenants in this book? Or, does it mean that Israel is united as one nation to fight her enemies as they have done over the ages? Let us try to understand the differences between covenant and promise. A covenant is swearing an oath which you cannot break. If you break an oath, you call down a curse of death upon yourself. (E.g. when Abraham made a covenant with God, he sacrificed animals, cut them in two, and walked between the pieces (Genesis 15). The gesture signifies that if I fail to keep the covenant, this may be done to me.)

The idea of Old Testament, or covenant, is to point Israel to the direction of heavenly rest promised by Jesus himself as he establishes the eternal and everlasting covenant through the shedding of his blood once and for all. Remember the Old Covenant (Moses) could not forgive sins, but only atoned them so Israel still needed a savior or redeemer for their salvation. We mentioned earlier that he who was born after the flesh persecuted him that was born after the spirit. Notice that Jesus was crucified by the Romans, who were the descendants of Esau and Ishmael, but he was given up by the Jews. Now, let us look at where this savior or redeemer is going to come from. Jacob, the twin brother of Esau, was a very cunning and tricky man and decided to trick his older brother of his birth right. With the help of his mother Rebekkah, who loved him so much, he was able to convince him and obtained the birth right from Esau. Notice that Isaac loved Esau and Rebekkah loved Jacob. As a result of this incident, Esau got angry at his brother and promised to kill him after his father dies. So Rebekkah helped Jacob to run away and go to her brother's house in Haran, but before he went away his father Isaac blessed him, "Let people serve thee and nations bow down to thee, be Lord over thy brethren and let thy mother's son bow down to thee. Cursed be everyone that curseth thee, and blessed be he that blesseth thee."

At Laban's house, Jacob fell in love with one of his daughters which led to marrying two of them, Leah and Rachel, and then he was given a maid for each of them for assistance. So the family of Jacob (Israel) from which the tribes came originated in North Syria during Jacob's stay at Haran with Laban, his uncle. Eleven of the twelve sons were born in Haran while the twelfth, Benjamin, was born after Jacob returned to Canaan. You can see their names and their mother's names in Genesis 29:31-35 and Genesis 30:1-24.

Jacob had one daughter, Leah's, last born, and whose name was Dinah. She went up to see the daughters of the land and when Shechem, the son of Hamor the Hivitte, prince of the country, saw her, he took her and lay with her and defiled her:

And his soul clave unto Dinah and loved her and spoke kindly unto her. And Shechem spoke to his father and said, "Get me this damsel for wife." Jacob heard that he had defiled Dina his daughter and his sons were out in the field with cattle and Jacob held his peace until they came home. And Hamor the father of Shechem went out unto Jacob to commune with him. And the sons of Jacob came out of the field when they heard it. They were grieved and they were very wroth because he had brought folly in Israel in laying with Jacob's daughter. This thing should not be done. And Hamor communed with them saying, The soul of my son, Shechem, longeth for your daughter. I pray you give her him to wife. And make ye marriages with us and give your daughters and take our daughters unto you and you shall dwell with us and the Lord shall be before you. Dwell and trade you therein."

And Shechem said unto her father and unto her brethren, "Let me find grace in your eyes and what you shall say unto me I will give. Ask me never so much dowry and gift and I will give according as you shall say unto me but give me the damsel to wife.

And the sons of Jacob answered Shechem and Hamor his father deceitfully and said, Because he had defiled Dinah their sister. And they said unto them, we cannot do this thing to give our sister to one that is uncircumcised for that were

4

reproach to us. But in this will we consent unto you, if you shall be as we that every male be circumcised, then we will give our daughters to you and we will take your daughters unto us and we will dwell with you and we will become one people. But, if ye will not hearken unto us to be circumcised, then we will take our daughter and go. And their words pleased Hamor and Shechem Hamor's son. And the young man deferred not to do the thing because he had delight in Jacob's daughter and he was more honorable than all the house of his father.

And Hamor and Shechem, his son, came unto the gate of their city and communed with the men of their city saying, These men are peaceable with us, therefore let them dwell in the land and trade therein for the land behold is large enough for them. Let us take their daughters to us for wives and let us give them our daughters Only, herein, the men consent unto us for to dwell with us to be one people. If every male among us be circumcised as they are circumcised. Shall their cattle and their substance and every beast of theirs be ours? Only let us consent unto them and they will dwell with us. They all agreed upon and all the male men of Shechem were circumcised.

And it came to pass on the third day when they were sore, that two of the sons of Jacob, Simeon and Livi, Dinah's brothers took each man his sword and came upon the city boldly and slew all the males. And they slew Hamor and Shechem, his son, with the edge of the sword and took Dinah out of Shechem's house and went out. The sons of Jacob took all the spoils of booty such as sheep, oxen, asses, and that which was in the city and that which was in the field. And Jacob said to Simeon and Livi, you have troubled me to make me stink among the inhabitants of the land, among the Canaanites and the Perizites and I being few in number, they shall gather themselves together against me and slay me and I shall be destroyed I and my house. They said they shall not deal with our sister as a harlot (Genesis 34:1-31).

CHAPTER TWO:

THE BLESSING OF THE FATHER

Jacob Blesses His Children

Dinah, their sister, gave birth to a baby and Jacob named her Asenath and took and dressed her nicely and put a necklace around her neck with a label written in Hebrew, "Girl," and put her on the side of the road where Arab caravans passed every day going to Egypt to trade with their merchandise. The merchants took the little girl and took her to Pharaoh's as it was the custom of the day. The girl grew in the house of Pharaoh and was beautiful. When Joseph, who was sold by his brothers, came to Pharaoh's house, Asenath was in the house as Pharaoh's daughter. When Joseph interpreted Pharaoh's dream and was promoted to second in command in Egypt, he was given Asenath for wife. (Genesis 41:45).

Joseph did not have to marry an Egyptian girl. He married a Hebrew who was his niece. From this story, we get one important point, and that is that the patriarchs of Israel could see the events of the future before they took place. Jacob knew that Joseph was going to need a Hebrew girl for wife in Egypt, as it was their custom not to marry from the Canaanite groups. Now, let us focus our attention on the future of the children of Israel, as we move on to the next step. As we all know that the children of Israel came to Egypt and Jacob their father also joined them, it came to pass that he was getting old and wanted to tell his sons what will befall them in last days.

In this section, notice the words of the father spoken to his sons, who I think were blessed according to their behavior and character. Jacob called his sons together and said, Gather yourselves together that I may tell you that which will befall you in the last days. (Genesis 49:1).

6

Last days could be interpreted as the last part of the tribulation close to the second coming of our Lord and Savior Jesus Christ. So pay attention to the words, "last days." Jacob tells them again in the second verse, "Gather yourselves together and hear, you sons of Jacob: And hearken to me Israel your father. In verse three he blesses Reuben the first born. "Reuben you art my first born, my night and the beginning of my strength. The excellency of dignity and the excellency of power. Unstable as water, thou shall not excel because thou wentest thy father's bed. Then defiled it, he went up to my couch." (Genesis 35:22). Simeon and Livi are brethren, instruments of cruelty are in their habitation. Only soul come not thou into their secret. Unto their assembly, my honor be not thou united, for in their anger they slew a man and in their self will they digged down a wall. Cursed be their anger for it was fierce and their wrath for it was cruel. I will divide them in Jacob and scatter them in Israel. You have heard that God loves the sinner but hates sin. Here, you notice that Jacob is not condemning his sons, but their actions and their behavior.

Judah, you are the one that your brothers shall praise. Your hand shall be in the neck of your enemies. Your father's children shall bow down before you. Judah is a lion's whelp from the prey my son you have gone up. He stooped down. He couched a lion and as an old lion, who shall rouse him? The Sceptre shall not depart from Judah, nor a law given from between his feet until Shiloh come and unto him shall the gathering of the people be.

Binding his foal into the vine, and his ass's colt unto the choice vine, he washed his garments in wine and his clothes in the blood of grapes. His eyes shall be red with wine and his teeth white with milk. In this verse, you see the greatest descendant of Judah is Jesus Christ. He is described here as a symbol of sovereignty, strength and courage, the lion of the tribe of Judah and he is pictured here as a lion in later times or last days. See Ezekial 19:1-7 and Revelation 5:5 reads, "And one of the elders said unto me, weep not behold the lion of the tribe of Judah, the root of David has prevailed to open the book and to loose the seven seals thereof." Pay attention to this verse as we go on with our story.

In verse 16, we see another son of Jacob come to the picture. We need to pay very close attention to this verse too. It reads, "Dan shall judge his people Israel as one of the tribes of Israel. Dan shall be a serpent by the way, an adder in the path, that biteth the horse heels so that the rider shall fall backwards." (Genesis 49:18).

"I have waited for thy salvation O Lord." (Psalms 130:5 and Isaiah 25:9) In Psalms 130, notice these words were said by Dan himself after his defeat by Christ in those last days. After he has said this whole chapter, then Israel remembered the words of Jeremiah 31:33. But this shall be the covenant that I will make with the house of Israel. "After those days," saith the Lord, "I will put my law in their inward parts and write it in their hearts and I will be their God and they shall be my people. And they shall teach no more every man his neighbor and every man his brother saying. Know the Lord for they shall all know me from the least of them unto the greatest of them," says the Lord, "for I will forgive their inequity and I will remember their sins no more." (Psalms 130:1-8)

Dan says these words or prayer, "Out of the depth have I cried unto thee, O Lord. Hear my voice and let thine ears be attentive to the voice of my supplications. If thou Lord shouldest mark inequities, O Lord, who shall stand. But there is forgiveness with thee that thou mayest be feared. I wait for the Lord, my soul does wait and in his word do I hope. My soul waiteth for the Lord more than they that watch for the morning. I say more than they that watch for the morning." This is Dan's prayer in Last Day.

Now let's go back to Genesis three and see the parallel on those two comparisons. Now the serpent was more subtle than any beast of the field that the Lord God had made. He said to the woman, "Did God say that you should not eat of every tree of the garden?"

And the woman said to the serpent, "We may eat of the fruit of the trees of the garden."

"But of the fruit of the tree which is in the middle of the garden," God has said, "You shall not eat of it. Neither shall you touch it lest you die."

And the serpent said unto the woman, "You shall not surely die. For God knows that in the day you eat of it, your eyes shall be opened and you shall be like gods. Knowing good and evil."

And when the woman saw that the tree was good for food and that it was pleasant to the eyes and a tree to be desired to make one wise, she took of the fruit thereof and did eat and gave also unto her husband with her and did eat. And the eyes of them both were opened and they knew that they were naked, and they sewed fig leaves together and made themselves aprons. And they heard the voice of the Lord God walking the garden in the cool of the day and Adam and his wife hid themselves from the presence of the Lord God amongst the trees of the garden.

And the Lord called unto Adam and said unto him, "Where are you?"

And he said, "I heard your voice in the garden and I was afraid because I was naked and I hid myself."

And the Lord God said, "Who told you that you were naked? Have you eaten of the tree that I commanded you that you should not eat?"

And the man said, "The woman that you gave me to be with me, she gave me of the tree and I did eat."

And the Lord God said unto the woman, "What is this you have done?"

And the woman said, "The serpent beguiled me and I did eat."

Now pay attention to this verse. And the Lord God said to the serpent, "Because you have done this, you are cursed above all cattle and above every beast of the field. On your belly you shall go and dust you shall eat all the days of your life. And I will put enmity between you and the woman and between your seed and her seed. It shall bruise your head and you shall bruise his heel." Notice the parallel between this verse and Genesis 49:17 that says Dan shall be a serpent by the way, an adder in the path that biteth the horse heels, so that the rider shall fall backwards. In this we see Dan as going against Judah and all their generations. Now we have answered the question about the flag of Israel containing two equilateral triangles which intersect one another in the center. This is a confirmation that we have holy trinity in Judah and unholy trinity in Dan. In John 8:44, Jesus tells the Pharisees that, "You are of your father the devil and the lusts of your father you will do. He was a murderer from the be-ginning and abode not in the truth because there is no truth in him. When he speaketh a lie, he speaketh of his own for he is a liar and the father of it."

Let us now seek more evidence from Dan's descendants, who may confirm the events of Last Days. If we go to Judges 13, we find that there was a man of Zorah of the family of Danites whose name was Mamoah. His wife was barren and bare not. And the Angel of the Lord appeared unto the woman and said unto her, "Behold now thou art barren and bearest not, but thou shall conceive and bear a son. Now therefore beware and drink no wine or strong drink, and eat not any unclean thing. For in thou you shall conceive and bear a son, and no rasor shall come on his head, for the child shall be a Nazarite unto God from the womb and he shall begin to deliver Israel out of the land of Phillistines."

Then the woman came and told her husband saying, "A man of God came unto me and his countenance was like the countenance of an Angel of God. Very terrible but I asked him not whence he was, neither told me he his name. But he said unto me, 'Behold thou shall conceive and bear a son and drink no wine nor strong drink neither eat unclean things for the child shall be a Nazarite to God from the womb to the day of his death.'"

And the woman gave birth to a son and called his name, Samson. He grew up and the Lord blessed him (Judges 13:1-25). And Samson went down to Timmath and saw a woman in Timmath of the daughters of the Phillistines. And Samson came and told his father and his mother about the girl and asked them to get her for him for wife.

Then his mother and his father said unto him, "Is there never a woman among the daughters of my brethren or among all my people that thou goes to take a wife of the uncircumcised Phillistines?"

And Samson said to his parents, "Get her for me because she pleases me. But his parents knew not it was the Lord that he sought an opportunity against the Phillistines for at that time they had domain over Israel."

Then came Samson and his parents to Timmath and came to the vineyards of Timmath, and behold a young lion roared against him. And the spirit of the Lord came mightly upon him, and he rent him as he would have rent a kid and he had nothing in his hands. But he did not tell his parents what he had done. And he went down and talked to the woman and she pleased Samson well. And, after a time, he returned to take her, and he returned aside to see the carcass of the lion and behold there was a swarm of bees and honey in the carcass of the lion and he took some in his hand and went on eating and he came to his parents and he gave them and they ate. But he did not tell them that he had taken it from the carcass of the lion. So, his father went down unto the woman and Samson made there a feast for her so used the young men to do. And it came to pass when they saw him, they brought 30 companions to be with him. And Samson said unto them, "I will now put forth a riddle unto you. If you can certainly declare it me within seven days of the feast and find it out, then I will give you 30 sheets and 30 change of garments. But, if you cannot declare it me, then shall you give me 30 sheets and 30 change of garments."

And they said unto him, "Put forth thy riddle that we may hear it."

And he said unto them, "Out of the eater came forth meat and out of the strong came forth sweetness."

And they could not in three days expound the riddle. And it came to pass in the seventh day that they said unto Samson's wife, "Entice thy husband that he may declare to us the riddle lest we burn you and thy father's house with fire. Have you called us to take that we have? Is it not so?"

And Samson's wife wept before him and said, "Thou dost but hate me and lovest me not. Thou hast put forth a riddle unto the children of my people and hast not told it to me."

And he said unto her, "I have not told to either my father or my mother and shall I tell it to thee? And wept before him seven days while their feast lasted, and it came to pass on the seventh day he told her because she lay sore upon him. And she told the riddle to the children of her people. And the men of the city said to him on the seventh day before the sun went down. What is sweeter than honey and what is stronger than a lion?

And he said unto them, "If you had not plowed with my heifer, you had not found out my riddle." And the spirit of the Lord came upon him and he went down Ashkelon and slew 30 men of them and took their spoils and gave change of garments unto them which expounded the riddle. And his anger was kindled and he went up to his father's house. His wife was given to his friends (Judges 14:1-20).

Chapter Three:

Judges for Isreal

God Uses Judges for Isreal

This story that we just finished, Judges 14:1-20, describes Samson's supernatural power that God gives him to fight for his people of Israel against its enemies Phillistines, who had dominated Israel at that time. This supernatural power will be demonstrated at the end of age by Antichrist, who will dominate the Temple of Jerusalem to judge Israel as we are going to see in following chapters.

And, it came to pass after a while, that Samson visited his wife with a kid. He said, "I will go in to my wife into the chamber."

But her father said, "I truly thought that you had hated her. Therefore, I gave her to thy champion, your friend. Is not her younger sister fairer than she? Take her I pray thee instead of her."

And Samson said concerning them, "Now shall I be more blameless than the Phillistines, though I do them displeasure."

Samson went and caught 300 foxes and took firebrands and turned tail to tail, and put a firebrand in the midst between two tails. When he set the brands on fire, he let them go into the standing corn of the Phillistines and burned up both the shocks and also the standing corn with the vineyards and olives.

Then, the Phillistines said, "Who has done this?"

And they answered, "Samson, the son-in-law of the Timinite, because he had taken his wife and given her to his champion or companion." And the Phillistines came up and burnt her and her father with fire.

And Samson said unto them, "Though you have done this yet will I be avenged of you? And after that I will cease?" And he smote them hip and thigh with a great slaughter and he went down and dwelt in the top of the rock Etam. Then the Phillistines went up and pitched in Judah and spread themselves in Lehi.

And the men of Judah said, "Why are you come up against us?"

And they answered, "To bind Samson are we come up; to do to him as he has done to us."

Then three thousand men of Judah went to the top of the rock Etam and said to Samson, "You don't know that the Phillistines are rulers over us? What is this that you have done unto us?"

And he said unto them, "As they did unto me, so have I done unto them."

And they said unto him, "We are come down to bind you, so that we can deliver you into the hands of Phillistines."

And Samson said unto them, "Swear unto me that you will not fall upon me yourselves."

And they spoke unto him saying, "No, but we will bind you first and deliver thee into their hands, but surely we will not kill you." And they bound him with two new cords and brought him up from the rock. And when he came unto Lehi, the Phillistines shouted against him and the spirit of the Lord came mightly upon him and the cords that were upon his arms became as flux that was burnt with fire and his bands loosed from his hands and he found a new jawbone of an ass and put forth his hands and took it and slew a thousand men therewith.

And Samson said, "With the jawbone of an ass, heaps upon heaps with the jaw of an ass have I slain a thousand men."

And it came to pass when he made an end of speaking, that he cast away the jawbone out of his hand and called that place Hamathlehi. And he was sore thirst and called on the Lord and said, "Thou hast given this great deliverance unto the hands of thy servant, and now shall I die for thirst and fall into the hands of uncircumcised?" But there came a hollow place that was in the jaw and there came water there out. When he had drank, his spirit came again and he received therefore he called the name thereof Enhukore which is in Lehi to this day. And he judged Israel in the days of the Phillistines 20 years.

Now, remember Genesis 49:16? Dan shall judge his people as one of the tribes of Israel. This chapter we have read Judges 15:1-20, which indicates the types of miracles and the powers he will perform in last days. This is a fore-shadowing of the last days with the Antichrist. His behavior is going to be exactly as Samson's. Then Samson went to Ga'za and saw a harlot and went in unto her, and it was told the Gazites saying, Samson is come hither, and they encompassed him in and waited for him all night in the gate of the city. They were quiet all the night saying, "In the morning when it is day we shall kill him."

Samson lay until midnight and then got up and took the doors of the gate of the city and the two posts that went away with them, bar and all and put them on his shoulders and carried them up to the top of a hill that is before Hebron. And, it came to pass those days, that he loved a woman in the valley of Sorek, whose name was Delilah. The lords of Phillistines came up unto her and said unto her, "Entice him and see wherein his great strength lieth and by what means we may prevail against him that we may bind him to afflict him and we will give thee every one of us eleven hundred pieces of silver."

Delilah said to Samson, "Tell me, I pray thee, wherein your strength lieth and where with you mightest be bound to afflict thee."

And Samson said unto her, "If they bind me with seven green withs that were never dried then shall I be weak and be as another man."

Then the lords of Phillistines brought up to her seven green withs, which had not been dried and she bound him with them. Now there were men lying in wait abiding with her in the chamber.

And she said unto him, "The Phillistines be upon thee Samson." And he broke the withs as a thread of tow is broken when it is touched by fire. So his strength was not known. And Delilah said unto Samson, "Behold thou hast mocked me and told me lies, now tell me I pray thee, wherewith thou mightest be bound."

And he said unto her, "If they bound me fast with new ropes that never were occupied then shall I be weak and be as another man."

Delilah therefore took new ropes and bound him therewith and said unto him. The Phillistines be upon thee Samson. There were liers in wait abiding in the chamber and he broke them from off his hands like a thread.

And Delilah said unto Samson, "Hitherto thou hast mocked me and told me lies, tell me wherewith you mightest be bound."

And he said unto her, "If thou weavest the seven locks of my head with the web." And she fastened with the pin and said unto him, "The Phillistines be upon thee Samson." He awaked out of his sleep and went away with the pin of the beam and with the web. And she said unto him, "How canst thou say I love thee when thy heart is not with me? Thou hast mocked me three times now and has not told me wherein your great strength lieth. It came to pass when she pressed him daily with her words and urged him so that his soul was waxed unto death.

He told her all his heart and said unto her, "There has not come a razor upon my head for I have been a Nazarite unto God from my mother's womb. If I be shaven, then my strength will go from me and I will become weak and be like any other man."

And, when Delilah, saw that he had told her all his heart, she called and sent for the lords of the Phillistines saying, "Come up one more time for he has showed me all his heart." Then the lords of Phillistines came up unto her and brought money in their hands. And she made him sleep upon her knees and she called for a man and she caused him to shave off the seven locks of his head and she began to afflict him and his strength went away from him. And she said, "The Phillistines be upon thee Samson, and he awoke out of his sleep and said, I will go out as at other times before and shake myself." And he wist not that the Lord has departed from him. But the Phillistines took him and put out his eyes and brought him down to Ga'za and bound him with fetters of brass and he did grind in the prison house. Then the hair on his head began to grow again after a while.

Then the lords of Phillistines gathered themselves together to offer a sacrifice to their God Da'gon and to rejoice for they said, "Our God has delivered Samson our enemy into our hand."

When the people saw him, they praised their God for they said, "Our God has delivered unto our hands our enemy and the destroyer of our country, which slew many of us."

It came to pass when their hearts were merry that they said, "Call for Samson that he may make us sport." They called for Samson out of the prison house and he made them sport and they set him between the pillars.

Samson said to the lad that held him by the hand, "Suffer me that I may feel the pillars whereupon the house standeth that I may lean upon them." Now the house was full of men and women and all the lords of the Phillistines were there and there were upon the roof about 3,000 men and women that beheld while Samson made sport. And Samson called unto the Lord and said, "O Lord God remember me, I pray thee and strengthen me. I pray thee only this time. O God that I may be at once avenged of the Phillistines for my two eyes." And Samson took hold of the two middle pillars upon which the house

---

Note:
Nazarite – separated or dedicated.

Zorah – a town first assigned to Judah by Joshua but later given to Dan (Joshua 19:41). This town became a point of departure for the Danites migration to the north.

Seven braids on Samson's head – symbolizing completeness, fullness, or perfection.

Da'gon – Phillistines God who Dan's descendants worshipped and served.

---

stood and on which it was borne up of the one with his right hand and of the other with his left. And Samson said, "Let me die with the Phillistines," and he bowed himself with all his might and the house fell upon the lords and upon all the people that were therein. So the dead, which he slew in their death were more than they who he slew in his life. Then his brethren and all the house of his father Dan came down and took him and brought him up and buried him between Zorah and Eshtaol in the burying place of Manoah his father and he judged Israel 20 years.

Since it was God who permitted their oppression and raised up deliverers, He Himself was Israel's ultimate judge and deliverer. Even Gideon, a judge, insists that the Lord is Israel's true ruler. The Book of Judges describes the life of Israel in the Promised Land after they left Egypt. It is an account of frequent apostasy provoking God their creator.

On the other hand, it tells of urgent appeals to God in time of crisis, moving the Lord to raise up leaders (judges), through whom he throws off foreign oppressors and restores the land to peace. In this case, we see Samson being raised to play two important parts in Israel. God appointed him to be a Nazarite, which means separated and dedicated to play both good and evil parts. The good part was that he was given power by the Almighty God to humble the Phillistines and stop them from oppressing the Israelites in the land. By his supernatural power, the Phillistines were afraid of him and limited their aggression against the Jews. The bad part was that he still worshipped the Da'gon, a Phillistines God since the Danites were still in the territory of Phillistines where they were observed and assimilated. Since they did not occupy their lot given by Joshua, they had no inheritance and frequently fought the Jews to obtain their inheritance. So because of their paganism mentality, they quickly forgot about their God and worshipped the God of the Canaanites. So the judge's time was the fundamental issue in the Lordship of God in Israel.

Only by the Lord's sovereign use of foreign oppression to chasten His people by implementing the covenant curses and by raising up deliverers when His people cried out to Him did He maintain His kingship in Israel and preserved the embryonic kingdom from extinction. Out of the recurring cycles of disobedience, foreign oppression cries of distress and deliverance comes another important thing, the covenant faithfulness of God (Neh 9:26-32). Nevertheless, they were disobedient, and rebelled against thee, and cast thy laws behind their backs, and slew the prophets who testified against them to turn them to thee and they wrought great provocation. Therefore, you delivered them into the hand of their enemies who waxed them, and in the time of their trouble when they cried unto thee, you heard them from Heaven and according to thy manifold mercies you gave them saviors, who saved them out of the hand of their enemies.

And after they had rest, they did evil again before thee, therefore you left them again in the hand of their enemies, so that they had the dominion over them, yet when they returned, and cried unto thee, you heard them from Heaven and many times did you deliver them according to your mercies. You testified against them, that you might bring them again unto thy laws, yet they dealt proudly and hearkened not into thy commandments, but sinned against thy judgments, which if a man do, he shall live in them and withdrew the shoulder and hardened their neck and would not hear.

Yet many years did you forbear them and testified against them by your spirit in thy prophets, yet would they not give ear; therefore you gave them unto the hand of the people of the lands. Nevertheless, for thy great mercies, they did not utterly consume them, nor forsake them, for you are a gracious and merciful God. Now therefore our God, the great, the mighty and the terrible God, who keeps covenant and mercy, let not all the trouble seem little before thee that has come upon us on our kings, on our princes, and on our priests, and on our prophets, and on our fathers, and on all thy people, since the time of the kings of Assyria unto this day.

The age of Israel's future following the redemptive events that came through Moses and Joshua is in a special way the Old Testament's age of the spirit. God's spirit enabled man to accomplish feats of victory in the Lord's war against the powers that threatened His kingdom. This same spirit poured out on the church following the redemption work of Joshua the second. Christ empowered the people of the Lord to begin the task of preaching the gospel to all nations and of advancing the Kingdom of God. Now, God wanted the nation of Israel to know that He was in control of His creation through the emphasis of His attributes of justice, truthfulness, mercy, faithfulness, and holiness. Thus, to know God's name is to know Him and His character. He is also the Lord of history for there is no one like Him.

He is glorious in His holiness, fearful in His praises, doing wonders. Neither the afflictions of Israel nor the plagues of Egypt were outside the control of God. Pharaoh, the Egyptians and all Israel saw the power of God. The basic evil and unbelieving heart and deceit were the standard for rebellion of the Jews. In the wilderness when Moses went to receive the tablets from the top of the mountain with God, people did evil in the eye of the Lord.

Aaron, the high priest allowed the children of Israel to make a molten calf be their God, since Moses stayed in the mountain too long. When Moses came down out of the mountain, he was very angry with the congregation. He dropped the tablets and broke them in pieces. It got worse when God found out about it. He told Moses to go down, "For the people have corrupted themselves. They have quickly turned aside out of the way which I commanded them. They have made them a molten calf and have worshipped it and have sacrificed thereunto, and said, 'These be thy Gods, O Israel which have brought thee up out of the land of Egypt.'"

At this point, God was tired of them and asked them to let Him alone because they became stiff-necked people and God was going to let them worship the Egyptian gods, such as bulls and goats, for the rest of their stay in the wilderness until salvation comes with Jesus Christ in his first coming.

Chapter Four:

Settlement in Promised Land

Disobeying God's Commands

When the children of Israel finally came to the Promised Land by Joshua, they were given allotments. One of the requirements by God was that they were to root out the Canaanites completely out of their lands. All men and women and children were to be removed or killed before the children of Israel settled in their lots. Unfortunately, not all the children of Israel were able to do that. Most of them lived with the Canaanites among them, which resulted in giving them their daughters for marriage and likewise their men marrying their daughters. They also, as a result of this inter-marrying, started worshipping foreign gods, which were not the gods of their fathers. They never kept the Commandments of God and that made God angry at them. The next thing was God brought oppression against them and delivered them when they cried for Him.

At this time, there were no kings in Israel and God had to raise judges to look after their affairs. Later in the years to come, God also raised kings and prophets like Samuel who appointed kings for them. Most of these kings did evil in the eyes of the Lord and they would have the whole nation punished as a result of their evil. Their first king Saul did evil in the eyes of their God and was quickly killed or killed himself and was replaced by David. He brought Israel the first organized government and the first dynasty of the house that God had promised. He also promised him the law of mankind.

In short, what Moses gave Israel (Torah), David will give the human race a revealed law of God. We know that Solomon became king after his father

David, the wisest and richest king thatever lived. But there came a time when evil befell him and he married foreign women women corrupted him just like the children of Dan. By the end of his dynasty, the whole kingdom was corrupt and finally ended in splitting into two, the southern and the northern kingdoms. Jesus once warned that the kingdom divided against itself cannot stand. So we see here Israel did not stand after that and they will soon be going to captivity in Babylon. Even though the prophets were raised to warn the kings and the people of their wrong doing, they still were not able to resist the foreign influence. They were taken to Babylon under King Nebuchadnezzar and then to the median and Persia and Assyria and finally to Greeks and Romans. This is what they called the wars of the empires or Punic wars preceeding the birth of Christ. By now God has demonstrated His authority and power over all His creation and also has shown His mercy and forgiveness throughout all the generations of the children of Israel. But the evil one the son of perdition is still able to deceive and lead man astray as we shall see in later chapters. If we believe and do not harden our hearts and seek salvation from the Lord our God, we may be saved. But, if we continue with the direction of evil doers, the road may be long.

God goes where we cannot go, and He does what we cannot do. He protects and provides both to good people and evil people because there is none like Him. He shows mercy where there is no mercy. He forgives where there is no forgiveness. He shows justice where there is no justice. And He is holy in all His ways. In Genesis 1:26, God says let us make a man in our image and likeness. This personality of God is a powerful personality. He is speaking to many and not one. This pluralism means there are other agents involved. Those are the seven spirits of God found in Isaiah 11:2. The Spirit of Wisdom, The Spirit of Understanding, The Spirit of Counsel, The Spirit of Might, The Spirit of Knowledge, The Spirit of Fear of the Lord, and The Spirit of Quick Understanding. If you take the seven spirits of God and put the attributes of God to it, then you have a God who surpasses everything in His faithfulness, His truthfulness, His justice, His grace, His love, and His holiness. With all these qualities, He is able to do all things. In Isaiah 45:7 He says, "I form the light and create darkness; I make peace and create evil. I the Lord do all these things." In Malachi 1:2-3 God says, "I have loved you said the Lord, yet you say wherein has thou loved us? Was not Esau Jacob's brother?" Said the Lord, "Yet I loved Jacob. And I hated Esau and laid his mountains and his heritage waste for the dragons of the wilderness. Brothers and sisters, who else can work with good and evil equally?"

When we fail to recognize our God or when we become ignorant and focus on our own ways, do we really know what we are doing? Apostle Peter in his second letter to the Hebrews spent a lot of time explaining to them how important it is to take the word of God seriously. Please read Peter 1:2. In chapter two of 2nd Peter, he lets them know that there were false prophets among them and as there shall be false teachers among them in the future who will bring in dimmable heresies even denying the Lord that bought them and bring them upon themselves swift destruction. Read chapter two of 2nd Peter also. Peter warns about the destruction that will take place in Europe in the years to come that will bring terrible destruction in the church and especially in Rome. 2ns Peter 14-22 describes their ways and actions:

> Having eyes full of adultery and that cannot cease from sin, beguiling unstable souls and hearts they have exercised with covetous practices. Cursed children which have forsaken the right way and are gone astray following the way of Ba'laam the son of Bo'sor who loved the wages of unrighteousness. But was rebuked for his inequity, the dumb ass speaking with man's voice forbade the madness of the prophet. These are wells without water, clouds that are carried with a tempest to whom the mist of darkness is reserved forever. For them when they speak great swelling words of vanity, they allure through the lusts of the flesh, through much wantonness those that were clean escaped from them who live in error.

While they promise them liberty, they themselves are the servants of corruption for of whom a man is overcome of the same is he brought in bondage. For if after they have escaped the pollutions of the world through the knowledge of the Lord and Savior Jesus Christ, they are again entangled therein and overcome, the latter end is worse with them than the beginning. For it had been better for them not to have known the way of righteousness, than after they have known it to turn from theHoly Commandment delivered unto them. But it is happened unto them according to the true proverb. The dog is turned to his own vomit again and the sow that was washed to her wallowing in the mire. Peter sees corruption in the church, in near future and is trying to warn Christians to be aware of such immorality which is about to come.

In the 10th century in Europe, politics began getting into the affairs of the church. Emperors started to take part in the election of popes in Italy, which they called emperial control. The masters of the city got involved in sexual immorality and treachery, murder, bribery, and war. The pope tried to bring peace, but it wasn't easy. The reformers saw the particular evils as the main weakness were simony the buying and selling of ecclesiastical offices, and the sacraments forbidden, from the earliest times. There were sexual irregularities in lives of the clergy and luxury in clerical dress. In 10th and 11th centuries and even dating back to 9th century, laymen became political and their power enabled them to abuse taxes and property. Bishoprics were a valuable possession because it brought power and financial advantage to its tenants for life. Even a parish with its farmland had a market value. Buying and selling were common evils in these days. Men held parishes and even several bishoprics and called it spiritual business. In such circumstances the standards naturally declined and it caused a lot of pain to good bishops in those days. The love of money became king of the world. At this point reforms were needed and some people began to do just that, but the emperors were against it because they benefited from it. Reforms were not working and things became even worse when two Italian popes were elected illegally. Anacletus II and Innocent II and this brought a lot of problems because they were both Antipope. Innocent put the whole country under an interdict forbidding the celebration of any sacrament except Baptism and Extremeunition and closing the churches and their cemeteries. They also stopped the distribution of bibles in homes of Catholics and in churches. This period of time was very hard for the church in Europe but we can't forget Matthew 16:18. The gates of hell will not prevail against the church of our Lord and Savior Jesus Christ.

In addition to all this confusion in April of 1378, Pope Urban VI was elected to replace Pope Gregory XI. Suddenly, there was division between Rome and France. Avignon papacy was already in place, but the Italians needed a pope in Rome. This brought the great schism or controversy which continued back and forth for 18 years between these two cities. By the year 1420 Pope Martin was able to select cardinals (secret college) to work with him in rebuilding Rome and bring the church back to Roman see the city of God. Several hundred years later, there came another protestor from a country called Germany. This young pastor who grew up in Catholic Church was Martin Luther. He was against the authority given to Peter by Christ and started Reformation to be set free to worship as he saw the church in his view. He became very popular in Europe and was joined by people like John Cavin, John Huss, William Tydel, Jacobus Aminian, and many others who supported Luther's ideas. Several years later, the church in Europe was split and today we have over 200 denominations on planet Earth.

What did Christ and Paul teach us in the Book of Ephesians 4? He taught the unity of the Holy Spirit in the bond of peace. There is one body and one spirit, even as you are called in one hope of your calling, one Lord, one Faith, one Baptism. One God and the Father of all and who is above all and through all and in you all. (Eph 4:3-6). This part of the scripture is lacking in our churches today and that's why we are all divided. We know that this spirit that was given to reformers in Europe was for the fulfillment of the scripture. Even though they rooted out the corruption of unworthy popes in the church, they also separated the church calling it Protestant and also ignoring the primacy of Peter in the city of God, which was Rome. We know that Luther had to play two parts as Samson did in the Book of Judges, and as the Maccabees brothers did in the last 50 years of Greek and Roman domination of Israel and also during Christ's time because these chief priests who gave Jesus to the Romans to be crucified came from the family of Maccabees. So, when God allows such things to happen, it's according to His plan and purpose and the glory goes back to Him. Luther has been classified as a devil by many theologians including William Evans whose book The Great Doctrines of the Bible lists Luther in the section of The Doctrine of Satan, page 225. So, throughout the ages God has permitted the wars of good and evil and we have seen some of these wars in our reading. If we do our part and give glory to Him, He will give glory to us in the end.

Let us now consider the existence and the personality of Satan. The Bible is clear about the existence and a personality of evil called the devil (Matthew 13:19). Then comes the wicked one. The enemy that showed them is the devil (John 11:2). The Devil, having now put it into the heart of Judas, Simone's son to betray him (Jude 1:6). And the angels that left their own habitation and kept not their first estate, he has reserved in everlasting chains under darkness into the judgment of the great day. (John 8:44). You are of your father the devil, and the lusts of your father you will do. He was a murderer from the beginning, and abode not in the truth because there is no truth in him. When he speaks a lie, he speaks of his own for he is a liar and the father of it.

(1st John 3:8) He that commits sin is of the Devil for the Devil sinned from the beginning. He had the power over death and is the prince of this world. In the Book of Job, chapters one and two, we see the personality of the Devil. He is as much a person as the son of God. In all these scriptures the attributes and qualities of personality are described to him.

Our temptations may come from three sources, the world, the flesh, and the Devil. That old serpent, the devil has spoken with fatal eloquence to every one of us no doubt and I do not need a dissertation from the naturalist on the construction of a serpent's mouth to prove it. Daniel 10 shows that Satan has power to oppose one of the chief angels because he is the prince of this world. He is the spirit that worketh in the children of disobedience. He is also the prince of the demons or fallen angels. The world of the evil spirits is now organized and Satan is the head of it. In whom the God of this world has blinded the minds of them which believe not. He is the prince of this world. He is not only the object of the world's worship, but also the moving spirit of its godless activities. He heads the kingdom that is hostile to the kingdom of God and of Christ. He has the sovereignty over the realm of death.

We have to resist him because he comes as a roaring lion to try to devour who is not sober or vigilant. To resist him, be steadfast in the faith (James 4:7). Resist the devil and he will flee from you. This resistance is best accomplished by submitting to God and by putting a whole armor of God (Eph 6:10-20). In order for us to be saved from sin, we have to obtain salvation. And in order to obtain salvation, we have to repeat and obtain knowledge of God and the understanding of God which comes by abiding in Him and Him in you. Stay in church and have communion with other Christians. The supreme business of God in this age, in the gathering of the church. Some day it will be complete and purpose will be served. For the perfecting of the saints, for the work of ministry, for the edifying of the body in Christ. Until we all come in the unity of the faith, and of the knowledge of the son of God, unto a perfect man, unto the measure of the stature of the fullness of Christ (Eph 4:12-13).

The time is coming when we will have no time to think about our actions in this world. When the enemies of God's people will arise to oppose the second coming of our Lord Jesus Christ. In John 14:3 Jesus is coming for us and not we go to him. I will come again and receive you unto myself. For the Lord himself shall descend from Heaven with a shout, with the voice of arch-angel and with the trump of God and the dead in Christ shall rise first. Therefore let us not sleep as do others but let us watch and be sober. For they that sleep, sleep in the night, and they that be drunken are drunken in the night. But let us who are of the day be sober, putting on the breastplate of faith and love, and for a helmet, the hope of salvation. For God has not appointed us to wrath but to obtain salvation by our Lord Jesus Christ. Therefore brothers and sisters, let us be sober so that we can recognize the man of sin when he appears to make war with the people of God. He is coming soon before our Lord appears. Death was destroyed by the death of high priest who is Jesus Christ our Lord and Savior. The New Testament takes the existence of angels for granted. Also the New Testament takes the existence of devils for granted too. In our Christian teaching devils are angelic beings that have used their free will to reject and rebel against God. The greatest of these is known as Satan, or simply the Devil. In their rejection of Him who is always love, devils have become utterly hateful and have twisted all their powers toward the destruction of creation and the seduction of the human race away from God. The account of the primordial disaster that befell our race through listening to such creatures is found in Genesis 3. It gives the account of how our first parents chose to try to save themselves from death of their own desires by trying to be like God, knowing the difference from good and evil. In making that choice to save their lives, they lost the life of God that should have been theirs and they therefore lost it for us. Thus we have lived in fear of death ever since. Indeed according to the Hebrews, the thing that subjects us to the bondage of the Devil is fear of death (Heb 2:15). Since our first parents sinned and put us in a situation whereby we all bear their sins, we need to seek salvation to remove this original sin from us which is given freely by Jesus Christ.

CHAPTER FIVE:

DANIEL TELLS ABOUT LAST DAYS

What we have witnessed by Samson's mighty strength, power and lies to Philistines and their daughters can also be seen in the Book of Daniel 8:19. And he said, "Behold I will make thee know what shall be in the last end of the indignation for at the time appointed the end shall be (Daniel 8:23). "And in the latter time of the kingdom, when the transgressors are come to the full, a king of fierce countenance and understanding dark sentences shall stand up and his power shall be might, but not by his own power, and he shall destroy wonderfully, and shall prosper and practice, and shall destroy the might and the holy people. And through his policy he shall cause craft to prosper in his hand, and he shall magnify himself in his heart and by peace he shall destroy many. He shall also stand up against the prince of princes, but he shall be broken without hand. Does this sound familiar to you? Remember in the garden? This king who Daniel proclaims that he will come from the North is seen as powerful." (Daniel 11:36) And the king shall do according to his will, and he shall exalt himself and magnify himself above all gods and shall speak marvelous things against the God of gods and shall prosper till the indignation be accomplish, for that which is determined shall be done. Neither shall he regard the God of his fathers, nor the desire of women, nor regard any god for he shall magnify himself above all. But in his estate shall he honor the God of forces and a god who his fathers knew not (Da'gon). Shall he honor with gold and silver and with precious stones and pleasant things. Thus, he shall do in the most strong holds with a strange god whom he shall acknowledge and increase with glory, and he shall cause them to rule over many and shall divide the land for gain. In these verses we see true colors of Samson.

Notice something like: "Neither shall he regard the God of his fathers or a god whom his fathers knew not." They knew not the God their fathers because they worshipped Da'gon, the god of Philistines. Now, let us see what God himself says about the prince of Tyre in the Book of Isaiah and Ezekiel.

> How art thou fallen from Heaven O Lucifer son of the morning, how art thou cut down to the ground which didst weaken the nations. For thou has said in thine heart. I will ascend into Heaven. I will exalt my throne above the stars of God. I will sit also upon the mount of the congregation in the sides of the North. I will ascend above the heights of the clouds. I will be like the most high. In these verses, we see the Antichrist trying to take the throne of God (Isaiah 14:12).

In Ezekiel 1:1-10 Remember Ty'rus was the home of the Danites. Son of man God says to Ezekiel, say to the prince of Ty'rus, thus says the Lord God. Because thine heart is lifted up and thou has said

> "I am a God, I sit in the seat of God, in the midst of the seas, yet thou art a man and not God, though thou set thine heart as the heart of God. Behold thou art wiser than Daniel, there is no secret that they can hide from thee. With thy wisdom and thine understanding thou hast gotten thee riches and hast gotten gold and silver unto thou treasures. By the great wisdom and by the traffick has thou increased thy riches and thine heart is lifted up because of thy riches. Therefore thus says the Lord God, "Because thou has set thine heart as the heart of God, Behold therefore I will bring strangers upon thee, the terrible of the nations, and they shall draw their swords against the beauty of thy wisdom and they shall defile thy brightness. They shall bring thee down in the pit and thou shall die the deaths of them that are slain in the midst of the seas. Wilt thou yet say before him that slayeth thee I am God but thou shall be a man but not God, in the hand of him that slayeth thee. Thou shall die the death of uncircumcised by the hand of strangers for I have spoken it," says the Lord God.

In these verses, we find that God is responding to the devil demonstrating his power against the devil and imposing punishment on him. The Devil will never have victory over God. (Ezekiel 28:1-10) The God instructs Ezekiel to lament or pray for the prince of Ty'rus and say to him:

> Thus says the Lord God. Thou sealest up the sum, full of wisdom and perfect in beauty. You have been in the Eden the garden of God, every precious stone was your covering, the sardius, topaz and the diamond, beryl, the onyx and the jasper, the supphive, the emerald and the carbuele and gold the workmanship of thy tabrets and thy pipes was prepared in thee in the day that you were created. You were the anointed cherub that covered and I have set you so you were upon the mountain of God. You have walked up and down in the midst of the stones of fire. You were perfect in your ways from the day you were created till iniquity was found in you. By the multitude of your merchandise they have filled the midst of thee with violence and you have sinned, therefore I will cast thee as profane out of the mountain of God and I will destroy you. O covering cherub from the midst of the stones of fire. Your heart was lifted up because of your beauty and you have corrupted your wisdom by reason of your brightness. I will lay thee before kings that they may behold thee. You have defiled your sanctuaries by the multitude of your iniquities, by the iniquity of your traffick, therefore, I will bring fire from the midst of thee, it shall devour thee and I will bring thee to ashes upon the earth in the sight of them that behold thee. All they that know thee among the people shall be astonished at thee, you shall be a terror and never shall you be any more (Ezekiel 28:11-19).

Notice Ty're and Zidon were next to each other in allotment and God is against them in the following verses. Home of the Danites. In the Book of Ezekiel 28 that we just read, God is explaining the prince of Ty're (devil) and how he was created and everything given to him by God, but through his disobedience he lost everything and punishment came upon him.

Let us now turn to the back of Daniel and see what he says about the events of the last days. In chapter eight of Daniel, while he was still in Babylon, he saw many visions in his dreams. These dreams revealed to him what the signs of the last days shall be. In chapter 8:16. And I heard a man's voice between the banks of Ulai (River), which called and said, "Gabriel, (angel) make this man to understand the vision." So he came near where I stood, and when he came I was afraid and fell upon my face, but he said unto me, "Understand O son of man, for at the time of the end shall be the vision." Now as he was speaking with me. I was in a deep sleep on my face toward the ground but he touched me and set me upright. And he said, "Behold I will make thee know what shall be in the last end of the indignation, for at the time appointed the end shall be."

The ram which you saw having two horns are the kings of Media and Persia. And the rough goat is the king of Gracia (Greece) and the great horn that is between his eyes is the first king Alexander the Great. Now that being broken, whereas four stood up for it, four kingdoms shall stand up out of the nation, but not in his own power. And in latter time of their kingdom when the transgressors are come to the full, a king of fierce countenance and understanding dark sentences shall stand up. This is Antiochus Eppiphenes, which means God's Manifestation, who most theologians believe holds the sign of 666, the mark of the beast. The king's power shall be might but not by his own power. (Remember Samson?) He shall destroy wonderfully and shall prosper and practice and shall destroy the might and the holy people. Through his policy also he shall cause craft to prosper in his hand and he shall magnify himself in his heart, and by peace shall destroy many. He shall also stand against the prince of princes, but he shall be broken without hand. Antiochus Eppiphenes was the last of four kings mentioned by Daniel 8:22. These four generals occupied Palestine and their capital city was Jerusalem. There was a family of a father, three sons and grandson who revolted against these kings and refused their doctrine of foreign gods who were against the god of Abraham, Isaac, and Jacob. This was the family of Mattathias, who was the father. His sons were Judas, Simon, and Jonathan. The son of Simon, whose name was John Hycanus, moved to the mountains to fight these kings and defend their nation Israel. They fought hard and God gave them strength and became victorious against this Antiochus Eppiphenes. After their victory, they consecrated and purified the temple because Antiochus had already defiled the temple with the images of animals and other abominable idols which was proclaimed by Daniel 12:11.

It reads: "And from the time that the daily sacrifice shall be taken away, and abomination that makes desolate set up, there shall be a thousand two hundred ninety days. When the temple was purified and the normal sacrifices resumed they put menorah (i.e. seven candlesticks) as described by Moses on Ex 25:31-40 and they praised the Lord and called it "the light that shines in the darkness." Now we see after the purification of the temple, the family of Maccabees which means (Harmmer) appointed other devout Jews high priests.

This group of aristocrats separated themselves and named themselves the Pharisees. There were other groups of lower status in Palestine such as the Sadducees and Scribes. Also there is the Essenes of Cumran community around the Dead Sea where scrolls were found, this special group that focuses on serving God is where most Apostles came from and also Jesus himself. When Jesus spoke about the wheat and tears growing together, this is what he was talking about. Now, the last king Antiochus in Palestine before the Romans who elevated himself above all gods and occupied the temple of Jerusalem, also came from North (Syria) and gave himself a name according to the city of Antioch where the believers of Christ were first called Christians. The suggestion here is that he meets the qualification of a Danite descendant and therefore being serpent, by the way.

Another thing is that he defiled the temple of Jerusalem by displaying the images of his gods, who were not the God of Israel and by talking blasphemy against the God of Israel. He also stopped the daily sacrifices in the temple and all worships and services by the Jews. Thanks to the family of Maccabees, who firmly defended their temple and their nation. After this successful battle over the temple, they isolated themselves and it is at this time they were called Pharisees or Separatists and they were also called bandit or assassins. They practiced Torah, or the law, and did not tolerate people who interfered with their affairs. They would easily kill them without cause. As revolutionaries, they opposed any parties that did not practice the law. By the time of Jesus' birth, they were the leaders of society and occupied the high priest positions in the service of God. So we see the same high priests of the Jews denying Jesus and giving him up to die under the hands of the Romans. (John 18:24) Now Annas had sent him bound unto Caiaphas the High Priest. (John 28) Then they led Jesus from Caiaphas to the hall of judgment and it was early and they themselves went not into the judgment hall lest they be defiled, but that they might eat the Passover. Here it looks like the High priests came from the family of Dan because they stand as judges. Remember Genesis 49:16. Dan shall judge his people. (John 19:1) Then, Pilate therefore took Jesus and scourged him and the soldiers planted a crown of thorns and put it on his head, and they put on him a purple robe. And they said to him, "Are you king of the Jews?" And then smote him with their hands. Pilate therefore went forth again and said unto them, Behold I find not a fault in him so I bring him back to you. Then came Jesus forth wearing the crown of thorns and the purple robe. And Pilate said unto them, "Behold the man!"

When the chief priests therefore and the officers saw him, they cried out saying, Crucify him, crucify him. Pilate said unto them, "You take him and crucify him for I find no fault in him. (John 19:7-10) They determined that according to the law of the Jews, he has to die because he made himself son of God.

And the Pilate came to him and said, "Why are you not answering my question, don't you know that I have power to crucify you and I also have power to release you?"

Jesus answered, "You couldest have no power over me at all unless it was given from above therefore that delivered me unto thee has the greater sin." They delivered him to be crucified and died on the cross, buried but in three days he rose up and was seen by Mary Magdalene, Peter, and John the one he loved most. He later showed himself to the disciples at the Sea of Tiberias. When Jesus rose up from the dead, he conquered the Devil, who had no power over him and the Scepter shall not depart from Judah nor a lawgiver from between his feet. He is the lion of the tribe of Judah and his brethren shall praise him.

Now prophet Isaiah predicted the birth of Jesus in his book chapter 9:6. For unto us the child is born, unto us the son is given and the government shall be upon his shoulder and his name shall be called Wonderful, Counselor, the Mighty God, the Everlasting Father and the Prince of Peace. On the increase of his government and peace, there shall be no end upon the throne of David and upon his kingdom to order it and to establish it with judgment and his justice from henceforth even forever. The zeal of the Lord of host will perform this. Isaiah is here declaring that the child which will be born will be all the above and will establish a kingdom that will have no end. Nevertheless, he will be tried and tested along the way.

In Matthew 16:13 Jesus asked his disciples saying, "Who do men say that I the son of man am?"

And they answered, "Some say John the Baptist and others say Elias and others say Jeremiah or one of the prophets."

He said to them, "But who do you say that I am?"

Peter who they called Simon said, "Thou art the Christ, the Son of the living God."

Jesus said unto him, "Blessed art thou Simon Barjona for flesh and blood has not revealed it unto you, but the father which is in heaven."

And I say unto thee, "Thou art Peter and upon this Rock. I will build my church and the gates of hell shall not prevail against it. And I will give unto thee the keys of the kingdom of Heaven and whatsoever thou shall bind on earth shall be bound in Heaven. And whatsoever thou shall loose on earth shall be loosed in heaven."

This is the most misunderstood verse of the Bible and the most misconceived. First, we need to know who is talking, then to realize who he is talking to. What his mission is and who he takes the message to? The receivers of the message in this era (i.e. the Christian period) are going to make the mistakes that the children of Israel made in the wilderness. God, through Moses, made several covenants with the children of Israel after they left Egypt and dwelled in the wilderness. Because of unbelief and the hardness of their hearts, they broke the rules and walked away from their God often and went seeking other gods.

Somebody asked me in one occasion why we have too many denominations in the world today. My answer was: Moses went on top of the mountain to receive the Ten Commandments. When he came down to the people he found that they have already made their own god that they worshipped in Egypt. Similarly, the Christians today want to build their own church and make their own keys to Heaven. Just like the Jews never listened to Moses to keep God's Commandments, Christians of today will not listen and obey Jesus' words that he spoke through Peter. That's why we have many denominations in the world today. The point is, when you stop worshipping the God of Abraham, Isaac, and Jacob, you start worshipping the Gods of Philistines like the Danites and not the God of Israel.

CHAPTER SIX:

THE CHURCH

Gospel in Gentile Land

D on't forget that when Christianity was taken to gentile lands by Peter and Paul, there were the same sects in all Europe as it was in Palestine. Through Diasporas or dispersion of Israel began in exile in Babylon and accelerated during the Greek occupation of the Palestine. When the Romans took over Palestine from Greeks occupation, more Jews were leaving Israel and going to whoever accepted them in their land. Europe was filled with Jews who were cut off from the temple and concentrated their religious life through the study of Torah and meeting in the synagogues were used to the old Jewish customs of the temple worship. Therefore, it was hard to change some of these people because that's all they knew. It was so easy in Europe to start controversy or schism among religious sects.

When industrial revolution began in mid-eleventh century, the whole Europe was ready for change. The church was in the center of great controversy and that's when we started noticing divisions which some people call reforms. But remember what Jesus said in Matthew 16:18, that the gates of hell will not prevail against his church. The question here is what are the gates of hell? Let me tell you what I think they are.

The gates of hell was the Roman government that was about to crucify him in day time. Another gate of hell was the false prophet Caiaphas, the high priest who was about to judge him and give him to the Romans for crucifixion. Did they prevail against Christ's words? No, and this is why: Christ was crucified and died, but in three days he arose. Secondly, Christ instructed Peter to go and establish the church in Rome, the capital city of the Roman Empire. That means the Roman government cannot stop the establishment of the church in their land. It is still there the Vatican. The false prophets and the high priests could not keep him in the grave more than three days. He had already told them that he would destroy the temple and build it back in three days. Why, then, would anyone not listen and obey the word of God? As the spirit of evil overpowered the Jews in the wilderness, so did the same spirit overpower the Christians in the Middle Ages. As the Jews were taken to Babylonian captivity for their disobedience, so was the church taken to captivity in France. The point is as the Jews returned to Israel to their own land in due time, so will the church return to Rome in due time. If this does not happen before the resurrection of the dead, then our Lord's words are in vain. In the Old Covenant, and in the wilderness especially, the forces of evil kept the Israelites from obeying their God and following his commandments. If we are not careful, the same forces will keep us from obeying and following our new sacraments which were instituted by Christ before leaving this world. Brothers and sisters, Christ is about to make his second coming. He is not going to be without opposition but victory belongs to him. The man of sin or the son of perdition will be ready to oppose him, fight him and do blasphemy against him.

Earlier in our journey to finding truth, we discussed that in the years between the 11th century to the 18th century in Europe came what some people call the great schism or controversy. With the beginning of university systems and the rising of industrial age or revolution, Europe started to change dramatically. With the coming of emperors, kings and queens in various nations, life was changing also in different aspects. The church was in the middle of it all because these changes affected the way they did business especially taxation and the whole church affairs. Because of these changes the emperors and government officials got involved in the selection of the popes in Rome. Some leaders would select whoever they wanted and not the one who met the requirements. In a short period of time, it became obvious that some popes started doing business, such as obtaining land and getting married, and the love of money became the order of the day by everyone. Corruption was growing daily and affecting those who were not in authority. So some university presidents around Europe, led by John Wycliffe of Oxford University in London, started questioning the authority of popes and bishops in the Catholic Church. They wanted to stay away from the authority of pope in Europe because everybody in the church was corrupt and did immoral things. Immorality grew daily and change was needed. For this reason, many people saw the whole of Europe going in the wrong direction and started protesting. They blamed the Church for everything and since the leaders of the Church were contributing to crisis of the society they began to question the faith of the Catholic Church. Many university leaders such as John Hus, John Calvin, and Martin Luther supported John Wycliffe's view of reforms. First they protested against some sacraments that were affecting their daily lives such as transubstantiation, the sacrifice of the mass and the real presence of Christ in the Eucharist. Some were against the tithes paid to unworthy bishops, some were against the celibacy because they wanted to get married because they said some of the bishops in the church had wives too. Some went against the penitent or confession because they did not want to confess their sins. So, the reformers protested and finally they were free to worship the way they wanted. The question here is who was right? The evil popes who they call antipopes or the reformers who did not observe all the seven sacraments as instituted by Christ himself? The Church in the world is still going through the devil's temptation because you can see how we are divided. Is there any hope for the church? The Church will have victory when Christ returns in his second coming and the Devil is defeated.

Just remember that you cannot win a victory until you defeat the enemy. When Christ returns and wins the war of all against all then his church will be sanctified and purified. What you witnessed during the time of Antiochus Eppiphenes and the temple of Jerusalem in 130 B.C. and what you witnessed in Europe during the schism period (the 30 year war), you will witness it again when our Lord returns. It is the same evil spirit that will be in action to defile the children of God. The serpent, by the way, is against the scepter and the lawgiver. Don't ever forget that. The John Wycliffe and the reformers in Europe also rejected the principle of the Holy Trinity, meaning that he was disregarding the Book of John 1:1. "In the beginning was the word and the word was with God and the word was God." Notice the similarities between Antiochus Eppiphenes, who claimed to be God and the antipopes in Europe? Antiochus deprived the Jews their right to worship in the temple, took away all their bibles, and sacrifices were stopped. In Europe, the antipopes stopped the distribution of bibles in the church and the families of the faithful, abused their positions by practicing immorality, sexual abuse, marrying and giving to marriages. Remember the days of Noah and of Sodom and Gomorrah? We see the same thing happening here and the Church was divided between the forces of good and evil. When Mohammed the prophet came to power about 600 A.D., he proclaimed himself a political leader, a religious leader, and military leader, making him King of Kings and Lord of Lords. He persecuted the Jews wherever he could find them. He forced people to convert to Islam. If they didn't they were killed. Jesus never forced anyone to convert to Christianity; he just preached the truth and let people judge for themselves. Mohammed taught that he was the last prophet sent by God but he was against Christ and his teaching. If he was against Christianity and killed the Jews people, then whose God did he claim to be? Watch out for serpents by the way. If your God is not the God of Abraham, Isaac, and Jacob, then you need to determine who your God is because Christ comes from this genealogy. Remember the enemy comes to steal, to kill, and to destroy. Don't assimilate to the wrong God or wrong doctrine. Know who Jesus is. In John 15, Jesus tries to make his disciples understand how to abide in him and love each other.

> I am the true vine and my father is the husbandman. Every branch in me that bears no fruit is taken away and every branch that bears fruit he purgeth it so as to bear more fruit. Now you are clean through the word which I have spoken unto you. Abide in me and I in you. As the branch cannot bear fruit of itself except it abide in the vine. Now accept me and abide in me. I am the vine and you are the branches. He that abides in me and I in him, the same bringeth forth much fruit for without me you can do nothing. If a man abides not in me, he is cast forth as a branch and is withered and men come and gather them and cast them unto the fire and they are burned.

In Europe before the great schism, or controversy, they had one Church which James the brother of Jesus called universal (Catholic). Due to the lies of men of sin, many felt the need to seek truth and moved away and gave themselves different names and started practicing the church without all seven sacraments. Is this the branch that has cut itself away from the main vine? Let us take another look at Luke 15. The prodigal son asks his father to give him his portion of good so he can go spend it in a far country. He went and spent everything in a short period of time. Very soon he found himself broke and begging for food. After struggling to find food and eating with pigs, one day he came to his senses and remembered his father's house. He decided to return to his father's house and his father welcomed him, made him a feast and forgave him all his faults because he asked the father to forgive him. His older brother did not like it, but the father had enough riches for both of them. If the prodigal son did not return to his father's house to ask for forgiveness and to make peace with his father, what would have happened to him? Just like the main vine and the branches he would have been cast away and bear no fruit. The father will not go looking for them but he is waiting for them to return. These two parables are talking about the church. When Jesus was resurrected and before ascending to his father, he instructed Peter how to feed his sheep and how to gather them together just before he returns for the second time. If you are or know anybody who might have cut themselves from the main vine and they are only branches, they will need roots to supply food and water before they wither out and be burned for bearing no fruits. These are the sheep without a shepherd and sheep without a shepherd don't know their way home. Remember your father's house has not moved. it is still where you left it and your father is in there, return to him and he will give you rest. Don't be afraid to come back and show yourself to him. Remember he knows what you have done. He knows you and most of all. He loves you but you have to confess to be forgiven. You have to repent to obtain salvation and you have to proclaim Christ to be a Christian. The way is open and the door is open. Knock on the door and Jesus will open it for you.

Chapter Seven:

Blessings and Curses

Jacob Blesses His Children

Blessings and curses are another factor to consider when you are dealing with the Jewish people. When Jacob blessed his children, he gave each of them a share of his behavior and character. Judah was the most favored among Jacob's children. We find that, throughout history, the saviors would come from him. We also see that Dan was given the worst blessing among all his children, possibly a curse. In most cases, the one who is cursed is likely to rise against his brother who is blessed. It is just human to feel that your right and opportunity for prosperity has been taken away. The one who is favored is always happy and prosperity belongs to him. The one who is cursed is always sad and poor. He is angry at his brother and of course the father. He develops a bad attitude and that becomes his nature or his way of dealing with reality. When Dan was told that he will be a serpent by the way and Judah is a lion's whelp and the scepter shall not depart from him nor the lawgiver from between his feet, it is obvious that these two brothers will rise against each other from time to time throughout their generation. It is also clear that Dan was the son of Rachel's handmaid, Bil'hah, and Judah was the son of Jacob's first wife Leah. Isn't this enough to make two brothers fight forever?

Let us look at a similar situation in the lives of the patriarch. Noah, who built the ark had three sons, Ham, Shem and Ja'pheth. After the flood Noah gets drunk and Ham, the father of Canaan, sees his father's nakedness and tells his brothers about it. His brothers took a garment laid it both upon their shoulders and went backward and covered the nakedness of their father and did not see their father's nakedness. When Noah got sober and awoke, he knew what his younger son had done to him. He said, "Cursed be Canaan a servant of servants shall he be to his brethren." And he said, "Blessed be the Lord God of Shem and Canaan shall be his servant. God shall enlarge Ja'pheth and he shall dwell in the tents of Shem and Canaan shall be his servant." Here we see another thing about blessings and curses among brothers that contribute to love and hate at the same time. The will fight wars from generation to generation. In such situations, we cannot understand why God would do such a thing to His people. Sometimes we cause our own problems and the result is punishment but some people get curses without contributing to it like Dan. God's plan and purpose for us is unknown by us, but only He has control over all His creation. Ham's descendants have never recovered from that curse.

God warns Israel against idolatry. There is one thing that God hates and that is idolatry and serving other gods. He tells the children of Israel to stay away from such idolatrous people. He says to Israel:

> If there arise among you a prophet or a dreamer of dreams and gives you a sign or a wonder, and the sign or wonder came to pass, where of he spoke unto thee saying. Let us go after other gods which you have not known and let us serve them. You shall not listen to the words of that prophet or that dreamer of dreams for the Lord your God proves to know whether you love the Lord your God with all your heart and all your soul. You shall walk after the Lord your God and fear Him and keep His commandments, and obey His voice and you shall serve Him and cleave unto him. And that prophet or that dreamer of dreams shall be put to death because he has spoken to turn you away from your God which brought you from the land of Egypt and redeemed you out of the house of bondage to thrust thee out of the way which the Lord thy God commanded thee to walk in. So shall you put the evil away from the midst of thee. If any brother, the son of thy mother or thy son or thy daughter or the wife of thy bosom or thy friend which is as thy own soul entice thee secretly saying let us go and serve other Gods which you have never known you or your fathers. Namely of the gods of the people which are round about you, near you or far away from you, from the one end of the earth even to the other end of the earth. A certain man from the children of Beliah are gone out from among you and have withdrawn the inhabitants of

their city saying, Let us go and serve other gods which you have not known. Then shall you enquire and make search and ask diligently and behold if it be truth and the thing certain that such abomination is wrought among you. Thou shall surely smite the inhabitants of that city with the edge of the sword destroying it utterly and all that is therein and the cattle thereof with the edge of the sword. And thou shall gather all the spoil into the midst of the street thereof and shall burn with fire the city and all the spoil thereof every whit for the Lord thy God, and it shall be a heap forever. It shall not be built again. When thou shall hearken to the voice of the Lord thy God to keep all his commandments which I command thee this day, to do that which is right in the eyes of the Lord thy God (Deut 13).

Here we notice that one thing God does not like is to share his name with other gods, or for us to serve other gods except him. From the beginning, God has said on several occasions that there shall not be other gods but himself and we pay a price by entertaining other gods.

Samuel appoints kings in Israel after the time of judges and was God's representative in conducting all that was to take place. He acted the role of Moses in the wilderness and was the one that selected the first two kings in Israel, King Saul, and King David. He gave the definition of the new order of God's rule that began with the incorporation of kingship in its structure. He provided the covenant continuity in the transition from the rule of judges to that of the monarchy. Samuel established kingship in Israel which changed in the structure of God's rule. He called Israel to repentance and renewed dedication to the Lord and Israel was able to defeat the Philistines through God's providence. Samuel's authority as a divinely ordained leader at the same time provides evidence of divine protection and blessing for God's people when they place their confidence in the Lord and live in obedience to their covenant obligation. The people requested for a king, and God commanded Samuel to give them a king. This request by the people is considered a sinful rejection of the Lord. It constituted a denial of their covenant relationship to the Lord who was their king. The Lord had promised to be their protector and had repeatedly demonstrated his power in their behalf.

The king in Israel was not to use his own power and authority, but rather he was to be subject to the law of the Lord and the word of the prophet. This was not only for the first two, Saul and David, but all the future kings who would occupy the throne in Israel. The king had to be instrumental of God's rule over the people and the people as well as the king were to continue to recognize the Lord as their ultimate sovereign. Saul disobeyed the instructions of Prophet Samuel and God instructed the prophet to replace King Saul with a new king. However, Saul was not willing to step down but he was wounded in the battle with the Philistines and fearing capture he took his own life. Three of Saul's sons including Jonathan, David's loyal friend, were killed in the same battle. This opened the door for David to become king and his monarchy continued in Israel until they were taken captive by Babylonian authority due to disobedience and refusal to recognize the Lord their God. God was the ultimate ruler of Israel and imposed laws and commandments for all his people, including kings and prophets and other dignitaries in Israel. His instructions were to be followed by all who were in position of service. Those who failed to do that were replaced by those who listened and obeyed God's commands.

Is Israel going to continue to honor God and his commandments that they have often broken in the past? Is God still interested in them? Are his covenants with them still in force? Now that they have no Davidic king and are subject to Persia, do God's promises to David still have meaning for them? After the great judgment on the nation and the destruction of the temple by Babylonians, the future of Israel looked faint. All their rights were taken away. The temple in Jerusalem and its service including its book of prayer and praise which was the early edition of the psalms are supreme gifts of God given to Israel through Davidic dynasty. For that reason his account of the reigns of David and Solomon is largely devoted to David's preparation for and Solomon's building of the temple and David's instruction for the temple service with the counsel of God the seer and Nathan the prophet. God's gracious purpose towards Israel through his sovereign acts of election of Tribe of Livi to serve before the ark of God was of David to be king over Israel, of Solomon his son to be king and build the temple of Jerusalem and of the temple to be the place where God's name would be present among the people. These divine acts give Israel the assurance that her rebuilt temple in Jerusalem and its continuing service marks her as God's people who have been elected by God himself.

Nazarite vow is as follows:

> When a man or woman separate themselves to vow a vow of a Nazarite to separate themselves unto the Lord, He shall separate himself from wine or strong drink, and shall drink no vinegar of urine or vinegar of strong drink, neither shall he drink any liquor of grapes or dried. All the days of his separation shall he eat nothing that is made of vine tree from the kernels even to the bush. All the days of his separation there

shall no razor come upon his head until the days be fulfilled in which he separate himself unto the Lord. He shall be holy and shall let the locks of the hair of his head grow. All the days of his vow he not come upon dead body. He shall not make himself unclean for anybody and shall remain holy unto the Lord. If any man die very suddenly by him and he has defiled the head of his consecration, then he shall shave his head in the day of his cleansing on the seventh day shall he shave it. And on the eighth day he shall bring two turtles or two young pigeons to the priest to the door of the tabernacle of the congregation. And the priest shall offer the one for sin offering and the other for a burnt offering and make an atonement for him for that he sinned by the dead and shall hallow his head that same day (Numbers 6:1-11).

This is the law of the Nazarite. These conservative Jews in that particular area called Cumran community observed very strict laws to honor their God. They had to remain clean and holy all the time until the vow period is over. During that time, they had special spiritual power in them and could be demonstrated at any time if needed depending on the situation. The locks on their heads were seven in number and they symbolized special strength like the one we saw by Samson. This law of self-purification on the honor of their God was very common in this community. This is the kind of dedication God is looking for from us when we can serve him with all our hearts, with all our might, with all our souls, and with all our minds. This group of Cumran community also practiced celibacy in addition to Nazarite vow. In honor of their God, they considered marriage time-consuming, leaving them with no time to serve their God. St. Augustine, the Bishop of Hippo in the fourth century A.D. agreed with this law of Nazarite and he implemented it in the early church because he was one of the fathers of the church. So it was carried out by the church for hundreds of years and still some parts of the world still do. Jesus also in Matthew recognizes this policy. (Matthew 19:11-12) But he said unto them, "All men cannot receive this saying save they to whom it is given. For there are some eunuchs which were so born from their mother's wombs and there are some eunuchs which were made eunuchs of men and there be eunuchs which have made themselves eunuchs for the kingdom of Heaven's sake. He that is able to receive it, let him receive it." In this passage, Jesus is actually saying that not everybody gets the calling to serve God but if you receive the conviction of the Holy Spirit and are willing to resist temptations, then do it and become a Nazarite. You cannot serve God part-time; you have to serve

God full-time and all the time. Why do you think God spent so much time with the judges and kings and the prophets and now priests and pastors? He is trying to get his people to know him, serve him, and worship him. He has spent almost seven thousand years trying to get us to understand that. How much longer do we need? What other ways and strategies is he going to use that he has not used for seven thousand years? We have eyes and still blind, we have ears and still deaf. St. Peter in his second letter to the Hebrews said, "There are wells without water and clouds without rain. Brothers and sisters God is almost getting to his destination, his abode and eternal." If you are not there with him when he gets there, don't call him because he will not hear you and if he hears you he will not answer, it's just that simple. Now go do your homework so you can pass those exams otherwise no graduation.

As we continue to explore the field of curses and blessings with the people of God, we need to pay attention to this subject; this is where the whole truth is. One son was cursed and the other was blessed. God himself has spent a lot of time talking to the children of Israel concerning this issue. In the book of Deuteronomy 28, God says to the children of Israel:

> If you shall hearken diligently unto the word of the Lord thy God to observe and to do all his commandments which I command thee this day, that the Lord thy God shall set thee on high above all nations of the earth. All these blessings shall come on thee and overtake thee if thou shall hearken unto the word of your Lord thy God. Blessed shall thou be in the city and blessed shall thou be in the field. Blessed shall be the fruit of thy body and the fruit of thy cattle and fruit of thy ground, the increase of thy Kine and the flocks of thy sheep. Blessed shall be thy basket and thy store. Blessed shall thou be when you come in and blessed shall thou be when you go out. The Lord shall cause your enemies that come against you to be smitten before thy face they shall be against you one day and flee before you seven days and seven ways. The Lord shall command the blessing upon thee in thy store-houses and all that you set your hand on and he shall bless you in the land which the Lord thy God gives you. The Lord will establish you a holy people unto himself as he has sworn unto thee if you shall keep the commandments of the Lord thy God and walk in his ways. But it shall come to pass if you will not hearken unto the voice of thy Lord your God to observe to do all his commandments and his statutes which I

command thee this day that all these curses shall come upon thee. Cursed shall thou be in the city and cursed shall thou be in the field. Cursed shall be thy basket and thy store. Cursed shall be the fruit of thy body and the fruit of thy land, the increase of thy Kine and the flocks of thy sheep. Cursed shall you be when you come in and cursed shall you be when you go out. The Lord shall send thee cursing, vexation and rebuke in all that you set your hand on for to do until you are destroyed and until you perish quickly because of the wickedness of thy doings whereby you have forsaken me. The Lord shall make the pestilence cleave unto thee until he have consumed thee from off the land whither you go to possess it. The Lord shall smite with consumption and with a fever and with inflammation and with an extreme burning and with the sword and with the blasting and with mildew, and they shall pursue you until you perish and the Heaven that is over thy head shall be brass and the earth that is under thee shall be iron. They shall make the rain of thy land powder and dust from Heaven shall it come down upon thee until you are destroyed. The Lord shall cause thee to be smitten before your enemies; you shall go out one way against them and flee seven ways before them and shall be removed from all the kingdoms of the earth" (Deut 28:1-25).

Breaking vows after you have vowed or sworn or made an oath unto the Lord, you should not break it. You shall do as you said. Breaking vows provokes God to anger. Vows, oaths and promises that you make to God must be kept to avoid His wrath and judgment. Look at the faithfulness of God in Hebrews 6:17 where God keeps his promise by an oath. Wherein God willing more abundantly to show unto the heirs of promise the immutability of his counsel confirmed it by an oath. Therefore, if God himself can keep His promises by an oath, how come we can't do the same? All God wanted us to do is to acknowledge Him and recognize his mercies and love and faithfulness and truthfulness. Because of His love, He sent his only son to die for our salvation so we can have eternal life. God cannot lie. He is truthful and sincere.

Chapter Eight:

Confession and Forgiveness

Forgiveness is one topic that is hard to acknowledge or even to accept because we don't believe that a person who has done you wrong deserves forgiveness. If you do not forgive others, you shall not be forgiven either. The problem with this subject is that very many people don't want to confess their faults because they may be ashamed of what they did or afraid of punishment. Confession leads to forgiveness and forgiveness puts you back in good standing with the person you sinned against. Whether it is a friend or God, your confession is needed if you need forgiveness.

Sometimes you may defend yourself like Adam did in the garden. When Adam sinned and God confronted him about what he had done, he refused to admit it and blamed his wife for it. As a result of his denial, he was kicked out of the garden. So Adam lost faith with God because he refused to confess his sins, not because he sinned. In the book of James 5:16 He says confess your faults one to another and pray one for another that you may be healed. The effectual fervent prayer of a righteous man availeth much. Brethren, if any of you do error from the truth and one convert him, let him know that he which converteth the sinner from the error of his way shall have a multitude of sins. The only person that cannot be forgiven is the one that blasphemes against the spirit.

In the book of 2nd Corinthians 2:5, we see that the emphasis of forgiving is enforced. It reads:

But if any have caused grief, he has not grieved me but in part that I may not overcharge you all. Sufficient to such a man is this punishment which was inflicted of many. So that contrariwise you ought rather to forgive him and comfort him, lest perhaps such a man should be swallowed up with overmuch sorrow. Wherefore I beseech you that you would confirm your love toward him. For to this end also did I write that I might know the proof of you whether you be obedient in all things. To whom you forgive anything, I forgive also; for if I forgive anything to whom I forgive it for your sakes forgave I it in the person of Christ. Lest Satan should get an advantage of us for we are not ignorant of his devices.

Christ is trying to make sure we understand how important forgiveness is in his eyes and that if you forgive others he will forgive you also. Most Christians ask forgiveness from God before they go to the person they offended. It is appropriate even to God if you first go to the person you offended, ask them for forgiveness then go to God and confess. When you cause grief, pain, anger, and emotional distress to a person, you have not done that to God, you did it to a person and it is the person that you need to go to before you go to God. Any confession made to God before an offender confesses to the grieving victim is not acceptable to God. A good example is seen in Matthew 5:22-26, "But I say unto you that whosoever is angry with his brother without a cause shall be in danger of the judgment and whosoever shall say to his brother Raca shall be in danger of the council but whosoever shall say you fool shall be in danger of hell fire. Therefore if you bring your gift to the altar and there you remember that your brother has fought against you. Leave the gift before the altar and go your way first to be reconciled to your brother then come and offer your gift to the Lord. Then your gift will be accepted of the Lord. Agree with your adversary quickly while thou art in the way with him, lest at any time the adversary deliver thee to the judge and the judge deliver thee to the officer and thou be cast into prison. Verily I say to you, "You shall by no means come out of this until you have paid the farthing Jesus told the Jews at one point in his ministry: I go away and you shall seek me and you shall die in your sins because you wouldn't confess where I go you cannot come."

Two Personalities

In most of what we have discussed about the personality of Satan, we have seen in several occasions he has displayed two sides of himself. His ability to entice is one of them. The ability to intimidate is another. You can also say that he has the ability to manipulate, dominate, control, and finally condemn. How did all these characters such as Samson, Nebuchadnezzer, and Caiaphas the high priest have two personalities? It is extremely important to understand this part because the character that we are trying to identify begins with these personalities. In the garden where Lucifer was before sin came into this world was a holy place before God. Because he was thrown out of Heaven by making himself God as he served God in Heaven. He was a fallen angel and he used his knowledge, wisdom, and power that he used in Heaven to entice Eve into eating the forbidden fruit. God did not let him occupy his kingdom in Heaven, but allowed him to be the prince of the earthly kingdom with God being the overall sovereign of all kingdoms. He had evil spirit in him because he wanted to overthrow God who was good and loving. Since then, he has used that spirit to enter in some characters' minds to subdue the people of God. In the first few hundred years, he was able to convince the inhabitants of the time he was God and had to be worshipped. After Noah's flood story we see that his grandson Canaan was cursed and decided he was going to follow a different god who was not the god of his fathers. God always reminded the children of Israel not to worship the gods of the Canaanites. So the Canaanites worshipped Lucifer who became the god of Canaanites and God was against it. God has always told the children of Israel that he will give them the land of the Canaanites and has always urged them not to take wives from the daughters of Canaanites. So this Canaanite god becomes evil spirit who goes against the real God the Holy Spirit.

As the Canaanites spread out on the earth, they separated into small groups as time went on. These were groups such as Shimar, Eliazar, Elam, Sodom, Gomorrah, Adamah, Zebulim, Beta, Kenites, Kenizites, Kadmonites, Hittites, Perizzites, Rephimes, Amorites, Girgashites, and the Jebusites. All these groups occupied a large territory and the Jews mixed up with them and adapting their way of life and eventually under their influence worshipping their God. According to a particular group and time, they would have a name of each god to worship which was an animal, a mountain, a manmade God from a piece of wood, molten images, etc. When God tells the children of Israel not to mix with the Canaanites, he knows the personality of them being turned into worshipping the Canaanites god. He knows what can happen when they mix.

When Abraham was born in the Shimar of Mesopotamia where his father Terah was serving in the army of Nimrod the mighty hunter. After he was born, the father and mother hid him in caves to escape persecution by Nimrod just as Jesus was taken to Egypt to escape Herod's threat to kill him. Notice one of the reasons God asked Abraham to leave his country to go to a land he would show him was to move away from the gods of the Canaanites so that he would not be corrupted with foreign gods for he was about to discover his God, the God of Abraham, Isaac, and Jacob.

These Canaanites worshipped Bel the god of Nimrod at that time. (Jeremiah 50:1-2) "The word that the Lord spoke to you against Babylon and against the Land of the Chaldeans by Jeremiah the prophet. Declare you among the nations and publish and set up a standard, publish and conceal not, say, Babylon is taken, Bel is confounded, Merodach is broken in pieces, her idols are confounded, her images are broken in pieces." When they came to the period of judges, they changed the name of their god from Bel to Da'gon and again when they moved to the time of kings, they changed from Da'gon to Baalam. King Ahab the son of Omri ruled Israel in Samaria 22 years, but did evil in the sight of the Lord. He married Jezebel the daughter of Ethbaal the king of Zidonians and went and served Baal and worshipped him and his wife Jezebel was against Elijah the prophet of the God of Israel and made war with him and persecuted the people of God. You can see that they had multiple gods in their dwelling, but the God of Abraham, Isaac, and Jacob stays the same (monotheism) never changing his name. Now another test comes to Israel, the Queen of Sheba comes to see the King of Israel Solomon because she heard about his fame and wisdom. Notice how she approaches Solomon by cunning and enticing statements

> And when the Queen of Sheba heard of the fame of Solomon concerning the name of the Lord, she came to prove him with hard questions. And she came to Jerusalem with a very great train with camels that bear spices and very much gold and precious stones, and when she was come to Solomon, she communed with him of all that was in her heart. And Solomon told her all her questions: there was not anything hid from the King which he told her not. And when the Queen of Sheba had seen all King Solomon's wisdom and the house he had built (temple), and meat of his table and the sitting of his servants and the attenders of his ministers and the apparel and his cupbearers and his ascent by which he went up into the house of the Lord, there was no more spirit in her. And she said to the King, It was a true report that I heard in my land, of thy acts and of thy wisdom. Howbeit I believed not the words until I came and my eyes had seen it and behold the half was not told me thy wisdom and prosperity exceedeth the fame that I heard. Happy are thy men, happy are

these thy servants which stand continually before thee and that hear thy wisdom. Blessed be the Lord thy God which delighted in thee to let thee in the throne of Israel because the Lord loved Israel, for ever therefore made he thee King to do judgment and justice. And she gave the King a hundred and two. And the navy also of Hiram that bought gold from O'phir brought in from O'phir great plenty of almug trees and precious stones. And King Solomon gave unto the Queen of Sheba all her desire whatsoever she asked beside that which Solomon gave her of his royal bounty so she turned and went to her own country. She and her servants. Note: she stayed with Solomon for 3 years and went home with the seed of Solomon (royal bounty). It is interesting how she praised Solomon because of his God in verse 9 and how she gave Solomon presents. She was not praising the Lord of Israel but she was trying to entice Solomon to sin against his God. She was able to do that and also got more of her desires met (1st Kings 10:1-13).

This is exactly what we are talking about the two personalities. They come pretending that they are with you and for you but they are there to hurt you. Remember the conversation in the garden with Eve and the serpent? This personality which you can also call witchcraft has been used for thousands of years and still being used and still working probably better than previous years. In the 2nd book of Timothy 3:1-8 and the book of 2nd Thessalonians 2:3 state that the Apostasy or falling away period is very close, probably closer than we can imagine. When you take the Jews in the Old Testament and especially in the wilderness that never listened to their God and never kept his commandments that they were given, we wonder what's wrong with them. But when we Christians of today reject the word of God especially when Christ died on the cross for our salvation, they wonder what's wrong with us. Today we have made our choice who we are going to serve, how we are going to serve, and why we are going to serve who we serve. The gate which is as small as the eye of a needle has specific requirements which are already written in the book of life. If your name is not called in that last day, your name has been blotted out and the reason is apostasy. You defined your destination by the choices you made mentioned above.

48

CHAPTER NINE:

RESURRECTION OF THE BODY

In the book of 1ˢᵗ Corinthians 15:35, it reads: But some man will say, how are the dead raised up? And with what body do they come? In verse 51 it says that: Behold, I shall show you a mystery. We shall not all sleep but we shall all be changed. (52) In a moment, in the twinkling of an eye at the last trumpet for the trumpet will sound and the dead shall be raised incorruptible and we shall be changed. Some people call this the rupture and others call it the resurrection. Either way, this brings us to another topic of the man of sin.

When this occurs, the state of Israel will change dramatically. They will start rebuilding the temple because they are expecting their Messiah to return. This period herein Israel is the greatest tribulation which is seven years before the second coming of our Lord. Once the temple gets started, the enemies of Israel will start paying attention because they figure out that the God of Israel is coming back. They can now resume their tradition of worship and sacrifices as they did in the temple of Solomon. See the construction of the temple and its use in Ezekiel 40-47. At this point, there will be enemies of Israel coming from the north attempting to conquer Jerusalem from the mountains of Israel. Read about these battles in Ezekiel 36-39. Here they will attempt to negotiate for peace treaties which the enemy will sign with Israel for seven years, but as time goes on he will break the contract within 3½ years and start assuming more political and religious roles and finally occupies the temple. This leader from the North is Satan himself but he is acting as ordinary soldier. He is not revealed yet because the falling back has not started. He gets in the temple and stops all Jews sacrifices and takes away their bibles and orders them to stop worshipping their God. He starts talking blasphemy against the God of Israel and magnifying himself above all gods. He defiles the temple with graven images of foreign gods and proclaims that he is God. Does this sound familiar? Remember Lucifer in the garden? Remember that this is during the tribulation period and the gospel is being preached. (Revelation 7:4) And I heard the number of them which were sealed, and there were sealed one hundred and forty four thousand of all the tribes of the children of Israel. Of the tribe Judah sealed twelve thousand. Of the tribe of Reuben were sealed twelve thousand. Of the tribe of Gad were sealed twelve thousand. Of the tribe of Aser were sealed twelve thousand. Of the tribe of Napthalim were sealed twelve thousand. Of the tribe of Manasas were sealed twelve thousand. Of the tribe of Simeon were sealed twelve thousand. Of the tribe of Levi were sealed twelve thousand. Of the tribe of Isachar were sealed twelve thousand. Of the tribe of Zabulon were sealed twelve thousand. Of the tribe of Joseph were sealed twelve thousand. Of the tribe of Benjamin were sealed twelve thousand. Notice that Dan is omitted here. He does not take part here because he is the Satan making plans to judge Israel and he does not know the God of their fathers. The book of Revelation 12:7 tells us that this Satan called sometimes dragon was already making war in Heaven where Michael and his angels fought him but did not prevail and there was no place found for him in Heaven. Verse 9: And the great dragon was cast out, that old serpent called the Devil and Satan which deceived the whole world. Does this sound familiar? Dan shall be a serpent by the way? (Genesis 49:17) He was cast out of Heaven into the earth and his angels were cast out with him. He continues to fight the people of God and those who worshipped the God of Israel. (Rev 13:5) And there was given unto him a mouth speaking great things and blasphemies and power was given to him to continue forty and two months. And he opened his mouth in blasphemy against God to blaspheme his name and his tabernacle and them that dwell in Heaven. This beast was given power even to make war against the saints and all nations and tongues and overcome them. Read Revelation 12 and 13. In Revelation 14:1, And I looked, and lo, a lamb stood on the Mount Sion and with him a hundred and forty and four thousand having his father's name written in their foreheads (without Dan). (Revelation 16:13) And I saw three unclean spirits like frogs come out of the mouth of the dragon and out of the mouth of the beast, and out of the false prophet. For, they are the spirits of devils, working miracles which go forth unto the Kings of the earth and of the whole world to gather them to the battle of that great day of God, Almighty. (16) And he gathered them together into a place called in the Hebrew Ar-ma-geddon. This is where the great war is supposed to take place and where the great Babylon is going to fall. And when that great city fell, a mighty angel took a millstone and cast it into the sea saying,

Thus with violence shall that great city Babylon be thrown down and shall be found no more at all. Here we see that the great city has fallen and its Kings. And the four and twenty elders and the four beasts fell down and worshipped God that sat on the throne, saying, Amen Alleluia. This war is fought by all the enemies of Israel who come against them in those days. Israel for some reason was hated by her neighbors for centuries and they often rose against them from time to time either because they wanted their land or because they were against their God. For that reason Israel would resist this aggression and would fight back. This time will be the same and the result would be all nations on earth will come against them and only Christ will calm them down.

The disciples asked Jesus in Matthew 24, When the end comes, what shall be the signs? And he said to them, Take heed that no man deceive you for many shall come in my name saying I am Christ and shall deceive many. And you shall hear wars and rumors of wars, see that you be not troubled for all these things must come to pass but the end is not yet. And many false prophets shall rise, and shall deceive many. And therefore when you shall see the abomination of desolation spoken of by the prophet Daniel, stand in the holy place. Whoever reads let him understand. Prophet Daniel predicted two accounts of abomination of desolation. One by Antiochus Eppiphenes in about 130 BC and another one in the end of age by the King of the North. We have already seen in the book of Revelation that this king has already come and has proclaimed himself God. In the book of 2nd Thesalonians 2:3, Let no man deceive you by any means for that day shall not come except there come a falling away first, and that man of sin be revealed, the son of perdition. Who opposes and exalteth himself above all that is called God or who is worshipped, so that he as God sitteth in the temple of God showing himself that he is God. Here we see that he is ready to do judgment on his people Israel as father Jacob said in Genesis 49:16, Dan will judge his people as one of the tribes of Israel.

In Revelation 19:11:

> And I saw Heaven opened and behold a white horse, and he that sat upon him was called faithful and true and in righteousness he does judge and make war. His eyes were as flame of fire, and on his head were many crowns, and he had a name written, that no man knew but he himself. And he was dressed with a vesture dipped in blood, and his name is called, The Word of God. And the armies which were in Heaven followed him upon white horses, clothed in white, fine and clean linen. And out of his mouth goes a sharp sword that with it he should smite the nations and shall rule them with

51

a rod of iron and treadeth the winepress of the fierceness and wrath of Almighty God. And he has on his vesture and on his thigh a name written: King of Kings and Lord of Lords.

This here describes Judah in Genesis 49:8-12. We notice here that Jesus is riding on a white horse and the serpent is ready to bite the horse's heels so that the rider shall fall backward. After everything is said and done, the serpent will not prevail against the lion of the tribe of Judah and he will have to give up the kingdom to Judah forever and ever. How does he give or surrender the kingdom to Judah? By recognizing the God of Israel and doing away with the god of Philistine Da'gon. Now Dan gets down on his knees and praises the God of Israel"

I have waited for thy salvation O Lord. (Genesis 49:18) Then he goes to full prayer in PS 130. A song of degrees: Out of the depths have I cried unto thee, O Lord. Lord hear my voice, let thine ears be attentive to the voice of my supplications. If thou, Lord shouldest mark inequities O Lord who shall stand? But there is forgiveness with thee, that thou mayest be feared.

I have waited for the Lord my soul does wait in his word do I hope. My soul waiteth for the Lord more than they that wait for the morning. I say more than they that watch for the morning. Let Israel hope in the Lord for with the Lord there is mercy and with him is plenteous redemption. And he shall redeem Israel from all his inequities. In Isaiah 25:9, Israel continues with her prayer. And it shall be said in that day, Lo, this is our God we have waited for him and he will save us, this is the Lord, we have waited for him, we will be glad and rejoice for his salvation. God hears the prayer of Israel and says: But this shall be the covenant that I will make with the house of Israel. After those days, saith the Lord, I will put my law in their inward parts and write them in their hearts and I will be their God and they shall be my people.

And they shall teach no more every man his neighbor, and every man his brother saying Know the Lord, for they shall all know me from the least of them unto the greatest of them, saith the Lord, for I will forgive their iniquity, and I will remember their sins no more.

God forgives Israel and the nation of Israel is restored and this is what Jesus came for the second time to do. To judge the living and the dead and to restore the nation of Israel. Now that we have identified the Antichrist and the kingdom of Israel has been restored, where do we go next? Revelation 21 describes the new Heaven and Earth for the first Heaven and first Earth have passed away and there was no more sea:

> And John saw the holy city, New Jerusalem coming down from God out of Heaven prepared as a bride adorned for her husband. And he that sat upon the throne said, "Behold I make all things new and he said unto me, write: For these words are true and faithful. And he said unto me, it is done. I am Alpha and Omega, the beginning and the end. I will give unto him that is thirst of the fountain of the water of life freely. He that overcometh shall inherit all things, and I will be his God and he shall be my son.

The description of that great city the New Jerusalem is given in Revelation 21:11-27. This New Jerusalem is planet Jupiter, which will come from Heaven to receive us after the last trumpet sounds. Remember that there is in the Bible the future ages. In the book of Ephesians 2:7, "That in the ages to come he might shew the exceeding riches of his grace in his kindness towards us through Christ Jesus." This verse tells us that there are ages in the future that we have to go through as we have gone through the earth age. According to John's eschatology, they include Jupiter, Venus, and Vulcan. In each of these ages, humanity will go through seven conditions which coincide with the development of human consciousness.

The human consciousness develops higher from one condition to another. For example, during the Jupiter period, man will rise to higher degree of consciousness which is called Christ Principle. Upon Venus comes the 6th state of consciousness which may be described as the inspired consciousness. The seventh stage, which will exist on Vulcan can be called initiative consciousness because man now has reached the highest consciousness of Christ Principle. This is when you can say I am that I am and this is the name of God. Remember Moses and the burning bush? God told Moses to tell the Jews, "I am sent you." Even though Moses had many doubts in his mind whether the Jews would believe him, he still carried his mission and message to them. He had to fight very hard to get Pharaoh the King of Egypt to let them go. After several plagues in the land he finally let them go and Moses had to take them across the red sea to the Promised Land where he had to deal with these stubborn people.

In our journey to conclude our findings about the man of sin sometimes called the Antichrist, it is good to pay attention to the key points that will lead us to the outcome. The blessings and curses that we have seen used by God to children of Israel or by patriarchs to bless and curse their children is key to their attitude and behavior after blessings and curses. The book of Deuteronomy 28 has plenty of those. Let us examine the original of such occurrences and maybe we can reach to a clear ending. Remember the history of Israel was written in advance meaning that it was written before the foundation of the world. Now let us look at Jacob's blessing of his children. He begins by asking them to gather themselves so that he can tell them that which shall befall them in the last days. Notice the language of the father. Last days means he end of age. Now look at the blessing of Judah in Genesis 49:8-12. Then look at the blessing or cursing of Dan in Genesis 49:16-18. From this point, we have one holy and one unholy or one righteous and one evil. In the flag of Israel, which sometimes they call the Ensign, the Star of David or the Burnner, we discussed the two equilateral triangles that bisect each other in the center. This is an indication that they will crash each other in war often in all their generations. In the same verses of Genesis 49, we find the serpent being mentioned for Dan that will bite the horse's heels so that the rider shall fall backward. Who is the rider in this case? The rider in this case is Jesus in Revelation 19:11-16 exactly as it says in Genesis 49:8-11. And in the same chapter the same verses we find judge his people for Dan and we find kingship described for Judah. Now let's turn our attention to Genesis 3:13-16. At this point we see the serpent by the way deceiving humanity and causing them to suffer for generations to come. In this case the serpent was cursed above all cattle and above every beast of the field, upon thy belly shall thou go and dust shall thou eat all the days of thy life. And the woman shall bruise your head and you shall bruise her heel. Here again we see the serpent bruising human heels as it is said in Genesis 49:17.

In the book of Isaiah 14 and Ezekiel 28, we see a good description of Satan and his deeds and we also see the location of his allotment by Joshua. Dan was given the land between Judah and Ephram, but was not able to drive the Amorites and the Philistines out of the land. So Tyrus in this case was the location of Dan's allotment. In these books God reminds Satan how he was in the garden of God, Eden, deceiving Eve.

We see another enemy of God in Nimrod, the mighty hunter who constructed the Tower of Babel to reach Heaven where God resides. Nimrod was from the tribe of Canaan who was just cursed by Noah his grandfather because of his rudeness and disrespect of his grandfather. So Nimrod from a cursed

Canaan wanted to elevate himself above the God of Israel. He wanted to put the whole world under his rule as one world government and became a dictator. Moving on down we come to Pharaoh King of Egypt who refused to let the children of Israel go. Pharaoh knew Moses very well because they grew up together when his sister Bitia brought the child Moses from the river. After Moses killed the Egyptian for messing with the Jews, it was almost 40 years before he returned to Egypt. So Moses and Pharaoh did not have a good relationship, but God was going to harden his heart anyway. After his heart was hardened, he became so evil and gave Moses a hard time with the children of Israel. So you can see evil is working so far when dealing with the God of Israel. After the children of Israel left Egypt and dwelled in the wilderness, Aaron the Livite and the brother of Moses made a golden calf for the children of Israel to worship as God after Moses took too long in the mountain of God.

Such incidents are good indication that the evil one is still against the God of Israel and is determined to continue to fight him. When the children of Israel finally came to the Promised Land, the biggest problem they faced was to remove the inhabitants of the land as God had ordered them to do. By not removing them, they faced a real problem of mixing with them and adapting their ways of life and eventually worshipping their gods and marrying their daughters. It did not take long before that happened and God was furious with them. In those days, Israel had no kings but God raised judges for them to govern the people. It was at this time he raised Samson the Nazarite. He had two personalities and he used them to perfection. He used his supernatural power that God gave him to intimidate the Philistines from oppressing the Jews people. His miracles, his demonstration of power and strength, his manipulation and whatever other witchcraft he was using used it into perfection. He saved his people from the oppression of the Philistines but he judged his people for 20 years as father Jacob had predicted in Genesis 49:16. He was from the tribe of Dan and we know what the Danites were supposed to do by the way. He also came from the North, the perfect location of the Danites.

One other king from the North, according to Daniel, was Antiochus Eppiphenes which means God's Manifestation. He came to Palestine a few years before the conquest of the Romans. He elevated himself above all gods and defiled the temple of God by putting molten images of Greek gods and stopping Jews sacrifices in the temple. He took all the Jews bibles and prayer books and ordered them to speak blasphemy against the God of Israel. This is what Daniel called the abomination of desolation. This king magnified himself above all gods and talking marvelous things to lift himself up as God. This is another character from the Danite group that is supposed to be the serpent by the way. The opposition that he met during this time as a group of three brothers and the father whose name was Mattathias and a grandson called John Hycanus. They called themselves Maccabees, which means "harmer" and they fought the Greek generals or kings for several years and finally defeated them. They sanctified the temple and brought it back to its original state and put candlesticks burning with fire (Menorah) and called it the light that shines in the darkness.

The problem was just like Antiochus they elevated themselves to the high priest positions and Pharisees which means Separatists a high standard class or aristocratic (proud) just like the Greek princes. They regarded themselves above all other sects in Israel. During Jesus' time, the same group was against him and his teaching and always wanted to kill him. At this point the high priests and the scribes gathered together and the elders of the people unto the palace of high priest who was called Caiaphas who judged him to be crucified (Matthew 26:3). Caiaphas was entered by Satan just like Judas Iscariot when he betrayed Jesus in Luke 22:3. In such instances you find how quickly Satan is involved in changing good intentions into evil to persecute God and his people. Now you see another quick swing in Judas and Caiaphas the high priest. Judas was one of the twelve but he betrayed the Lord Caiaphas from the Maccabees family, who saved Israel from Greek domination also judged the Lord for crucifixion. What can we say about these things? Is the evil one a real human being who changes in a matter of seconds to do evil things to the just? Can you see how quickly the serpent can bite a horse's heels so that the rider falls backward? This kind of thing playing double roles at the same time can only be done by people who are rebellious and use witchcraft or idolatry and stubbornness.

Few days before his crucifixion Jesus took his disciples to the coasts of Ciesarea Phillippi to ask them who people thought who he is and who disciples thought who he was, but when Peter answered correctly he made him a rock where he would build his church. And he also gave him the power of binding and loosing keys to Heaven. Jesus proclaimed the gates of hell will not prevail against his church. He was warning them how the Jews who will not convert to Christianity will attack the church and his gospel. We saw that happen to the church about 500 years ago in Europe when Rome was dissolved by Antipopes and irregularities in the church. The reformers fought hard to get things in control and bring the church back to good standing. Leaders like Luther and John Calvin, John Huss and others around Europe took part. After the crises were over but the church still struggling to counter reform, the reformers decided not to go with the church in Rome and asked for a new identity called Protestant. In the end it was so. They added more churches and called them different names as they wished and now we have several of them on the planet Earth. Here again you see double roles played by reformers just as Samson in the book of Judges or Pharisees in the time of Greek domination of Israel and the high priest Caiaphas who judged Christ and Judas who betrayed him. These double personalities who play double roles are the ones Jesus was warning the disciples about. The problem here is they never prevailed against Christ's church just like in the Old Testament they never prevailed against God. Some of the things that God allows to happen to us is for us to learn from them but a lot of times we don't get it. A good example here is when the children of Israel made images of God to worship a calf in the wilderness, God ordered them to continue sacrificing animals as a reminder of their stay in Egypt. They did not know that was a lesson to learn that they were not in Egypt anymore and they did not need the Egyptian gods but all they needed was the God of Israel.

God gave them the commandments and laws to reveal their sin nature and those laws could not save them from their sins. They failed to understand what they needed. They often went back to their old ways after being corrected either by God himself or other leaders, in this case Moses. When God speaks, listen and obey. Jesus said that the gates of hell will not prevail against his church and they didn't. (Matthew 16:18) Jesus in Matthew 24:15 warned his disciples about the abomination of desolation spoken of by Daniel the prophet about the end of time activities. First the gospel must be preached to all nations of the Earth and apostasy or falling back meaning that the Jews in Israel will go back to doing sacrifices and saying prayers in the temple of Jerusalem which will be constructed during the tribulation period. When you see all those things take place and the man of sin be revealed according to Thessalonians 2:3, then you know the time that Jacob spoke about, the last days have come. You will see the King of the North proclaimed by Daniel appear in the temple calling himself God lifting himself above all and will take over politically and assume religious matters and judge Israel. Thus the words spoken of by Jacob the father of Dan be fulfilled. But shortly after that Christ will come riding on a white horse as it is in Revelation 19:10-16 and destroy the man of sin sitting in God's temple who is judging Israel who is the Antichrist who is the descendant of Dan. And all the words that was spoken by their father will come to pass and the end comes after the Antichrist says verse 18 of Genesis 49 and also the whole chapter of PS 130 and Isaiah 25:9.

Some people have questions about the man of sin coming from the European Union. Yes, this could be possible also because the Danites immigrated to Europe and took or settled in the country Denmark. This country was ruled by the Vikings from 750-1035 CA. This country was monarchy from the beginning ruled by queens and kings and was a great power. The Vikings were shipbuilders and fishermen, but the Danites introduced agriculture by 1200 C.E. They began to keep animals for livestock and introducing economic systems, such as government and society, education, religion, recreation, and the language which became Danish or Dansk. Soon the country was given the name Denmark after the majority of population was Danites. They are a member of Europe even though they kept their own currency, instead of using Euro as those other nations of Europe. It is among the 10 nations united to form a union that will participate in world affairs when the world forms one world government. As we see regular movement of peoples in all corners of the Earth, anybody can be a member of any country. As a result of this movement, especially in Europe, the Danites could be seen mixing with other European communities. So the Antichrist can come from European Union but he will be a Danite as Jacob told his son Dan that he will be a serpent by the way.

CHAPTER TEN:

JUDAH - GREAT GREAT GRANDFATHER OF CHRIST

Let us now turn to Judah, who was given the greatest blessing by his father Jacob and possibly the biggest leadership role in the history of Jews people. Let us see how he defends his scepter and kingship throughout the generations until the last days. The scepter, which is also a star, and the kingship were perhaps fulfilled initially in King David but was ultimately fulfilled in the coming Messianic rule. Israel's future deliverer will be like a star. This scepter in his royalty will bring victories over the enemies of his people. His course of maintaining these titles will be challenged along the way, but he will defend them throughout the generations until the end.

Judah and Tamar: in Genesis 38 Judah gets his first test as royal King but through God's will he will overcome the adversity and come out victorious. It reads:

> And it came to pass at that time that Judah went down from his brethren and turned in to a certain Adullami to whose name was Hirah. And Judah saw there a daughter of a certain Canaanite whose name was Shuah and he took her and went into her. And she conceived and bare a son and he called his name Er. And she conceived again and bare a son and she called his name Onan. And she yet again conceived and bare a son and called his name Shelah and he was at Chezib when she bare him. And Judah took a wife for Er his first born whose name was Tamar. And Er, Judah's first born, was wicked in the sight of the Lord, and the Lord slew him. And

Judah said to Onan the second born, Go in unto her thy brother's wife and marry her and raise up seed to thy brother. And Onan knew that the seed should not be his, and it came to pass when he went in unto his brother's wife, that he spilled it on the ground lest that he should give seed to his brother. And the thing that he did displeased the Lord, wherefore the Lord slew him also.

Then said Judah to Tamar his daughter in law, Remain a widow at thy father's house till Shelah my son be grown. For he said peradventure he die also as his brothers did. And Tamar went and dwelled at her father's house. And in process of time, the daughter of Shuah Judah's wife died and Judah was confronted and went unto his sheepshearers to Tim'nath, he and his new friend Hirah the Adullamite, and it was told Tamar saying, Behold thy father in law goes up to Tim'nath to shear his sheep, and she put on her widow's garments off from her, and covered her with a veil and wrapped herself and sat in an open place which is by the way to Tim'nath for she saw that Shelah was grown and she was not given unto him to wife. And when Judah saw her, he thought her to be a harlot because she had covered her face. And he turned unto her by the way and said, Go to, I pray thee, let me come in unto thee, for he knew not that she was his daughter in law. And she said, What will you give me that you should come in unto me? And he said, I will send you a kid from the flock, and she said, Will you give me a pledge till you send it? He said, What pledge shall I give you? And she said, The signet and thy bracelets and thy staff that is in thy hand. And he gave it to her and came in unto her and she conceived by him.

And she arose and went away and laid by her veil from her and put on the garments of her widowhood. And Judah sent the kid by the hand of his friend the Adullamite to receive his pledge from the woman's hand but he found her not. Then he asked men of the place saying, Where is the harlot that was openly by the place way side? And they said, There was no harlot in this place? And he returned to Judah and said, I cannot find her, and also the men of the place said that there was no harlot in this place. And Judah said, Let her take it to her, lest we be ashamed, behold I sent this kid and you have not yet found her. And it came to pass about three months after that it was told Judah saying, Tamar your daughter in law has played the harlot and also behold she is with the child by whoredom. And Judah said, Bring her forth and let her be burnt. When she was brought up she went to her father in law saying, By the man whose these are, am I with child and she said, Discern, I pray thee, whose are these, the signet and bracelets and staff? And Judah acknowledged them and said, She has been more righteous than I because that I gave her not to Shelah my son. And he knew her again no more. And it came to pass in the time of her travail that behold twins were in her womb, and it came to pass when she travailed, that the one put out his hand and the midwife took and bound his hand a scarlet thread saying, This came out first, and it came to pass as he drew back his hand, that behold his brother came out and she said, How has thou broken forth, this breach be upon thee, therefore his name was called Pharez. And afterwards came out his brother that had the scarlet thread upon his hand and his name was called Zarah. (Genesis 38:1-30).

Here we find Tamar determined to obtain the seed of kingship like the Queen of Sheba did to Solomon in later times. Throughout the generations, the Canaanites tried to seek seed of Israel for royal or higher positions for they knew Israelis were God's chosen people. In Israel, they had special harlots that they called temple prostitutes or holy harlots and they were different from ordinary social class prostitutes. A good example as we have seen such as Tamar, Rahab in Joshua 2:1. Sinful woman in Luke 7 and MK 14. Mary Magdalene John 20, etc. This kind of thing was acceptable in Israel for God's purpose.

This son of Judah with Tamar named Pharez became the head of the leading clan in Judach and the ancestor of David. In the book of Ruth, we see that Boaz the son of Salmon who married Rahab the harlot in the book of Joshua begat Obed and Obed begat Jesse and Jesse begat David the King and when David was appointed King by Samuel the prophet he began to be mighty and powerful in Israel. In order to replace the first King Saul of Israel, he had to be appointed by through a difficult choice but the hand of God was with him. Samuel ,who like Samson, was set aside by God for special service was born from a barren mother just like Samson and his head had seen no razor and he grew in wisdom and understanding and God used him to deliver Israel.

When Samuel was little, his father Eli was a priest and always prayed in the temple and one day he put Samuel to sleep near the ark of God and the Lord called Samuel three times, but Samuel did not know it was the Lord who was calling. After the Lord called for the fourth time, Samuel responded and God told him that he will do things in Israel for those who have ears to hear. God promised Samuel that he will punish the house of Eli the priests for their inequity in the land of Israel. Samuel was asked by Eli his father what God had said to him and responded by telling Eli everything that God had said to him.

The Bible tells us that when Samuel grew up, he was with favor of both the Lord and also with man. And the child Samuel ministered unto the Lord before Eli and the word of the Lord was precious in those days there was no open vision. And all Israel from Dan even to Beer Sheba knew that Samuel was established to be a prophet of the Lord. And the Lord appeared again in Shiloh for the Lord revealed himself to Samuel in Shiloh by the word of the Lord. When the Philistines were going against Israel, Samuel spoke to Israel concerning their enemies because the Philistines had the upper hand on Israel. They wanted to know who would deliver them from the hands of these people. Therefore Israel decided to fetch the ark of the covenant of the Lord out of Shiloh unto themselves to save them.

Woe unto us who shall deliver us from the hands of these mighty Gods, those are the Gods that smote the Egyptians in the wilderness with their plagues.

Philistines smote Israel and took the ark of covenant and killed many men of Israel. Two sons of Eli and Phinehas were also slain. The Philistines took the ark of covenant to Ashdod and brought it to the house of Da'gon and set it by Da'gon, the god of Philistines. When they woke up in the morning, Da'-gon was fallen upon his face to the earth before the ark of covenant because the ark was the presence of God of Israel. So Da'gon and his head and both of his palms and hands were cut off upon the threshold, only the stump of Da'gon was left to him. So the Philistines decided to let the ark of the Lord go for they said, The God of Israel is sore upon us and upon Da'gon our god. There-fore, they sent the ark of the Lord to Ekron and it was in Ekron a short time. The people started to complain that the Philistines have brought the ark of God to them to slay them. But the Philistines decided to send the ark to Israel to remove bad luck from them. Have you noticed that the God of Israel has power and authority over gods of Philistines as we saw in the story of Samson? The children of Israel did put away Baalim and Ash'taroth and served the Lord only. They asked Samuel to pray to God to save them from Philistines.

And Samuel took a sucking lamb and offered it for a burnt offering wholly unto the Lord and when Samuel cried out unto the Lord, he heard him. Then Samuel took a stone and set it between Mizipeh and Shem and called the name of the place Ebenezer saying, The Lord has helped us. So the Philistines were subdued and they came no more into the coast of Israel and the hand of the Lord was against them all the days of Samuel.

It came to pass that when Samuel was old that he made his sons judges over Israel because they had neither judges nor kings. At this point, all the elders of Israel gathered themselves together and asked Samuel to give them a king to judge them like other nations. After he consulted with the Lord about their request, he was allowed to give them a king as people requested. So Samuel elected Saul from the tribe of Benjamin as their first king. Saul was a wicked king because he did evil in the eyes of the Lord and was replaced by David the son of Jesse. Here you see Samuel playing the role of saving Israel from Philistines as Samson did, but Saul who was wicked, did that which was evil in Israel.

When David was elected to replace Saul, Philistines were still powerful in Palestine and still wanted to oppress Israel and were also against its God. But David began to be a mighty man, and began to take the matters of Israel in his hands to protect them and to save them from the oppression of their enemies. And David started to fight war after war for Israel's sake. Then the people came to him in Hebron and all the tribes of Israel and said, Behold we are thy bone and thy flesh and when Saul was with us, you are the one who led us out, brought us out in Israel. And the Lord said to thee: Thou shall feed my people Israel and thou shall be a captain in Israel. Notice here he is being assured that the scepter will not depart from him nor the lawgiver from between his feet. He made a league with them in Hebron before the Lord and they anointed David king over Israel. He was 30 years old when he began to reign and he reigned 40 years in Hebron. He reigned over Judah seven years and six months in Jerusalem he reigned thirty and three years over all Israel and Judah. (Samuel 5:1-5) This confirms Genesis 49:8-12 and Revelation 19:11-16.

David brings the ark of covenant to the city of David Jerusalem from the house of Obededom where it was kept for three months. So David went and brought up the ark of God from the house of Obededom into the city of David with gladness. And it was so that they bore the ark of the Lord and sacrificed oxen and farlings. And David danced before the Lord with all his might and David was girded with a linen ephod which maked him a priest as well as King after the order of Melchizedek. Judah here maintains his title and defends his kingdom as he goes on through the generations. David however is not going all the way without temptations and trials and tribulations.

David defiles himself with another man's wife:

And it came to pass when the kings go forth to battle that David sent Jacob and his servants with him and all Israel to destroy the children of Ammon and besieged Rabbah but tarried still at Jerusalem. And it came to pass in an evening tide that David arose from off his bed and walked upon the roof of the king's house and from the roof he saw a woman washing herself and the woman was very beautiful to look upon. And David sent and enquired after the woman, and one said, Is not this Bathsheba the daughter of Eliam the wife of Uriah the Hittite? And David sent messengers and took her and she came unto him and he lay with her for she was purified from her uncleanness and she returned unto her house.

And the woman conceived and sent and told David and said: I am with a child. And David sent to Joab saying: Send me Uriah the Hittite, and Jacob sent Uriah to David. And when Uriah came to him, David demanded of him how Joab did and how the people did and how the war prospered. And David said to Uriah, Go down to your house and wash your feet. And Uriah departed out of the King's house and there followed him a mess of meat from the King. But Uriah slept at the door of the King's house with all the servants of his Lord and went not down to his house. And when they had told David saying, Uriah went not down to his house, David said unto Uriah, Comest thy not from thy journey? Why did you not go to your house? And Uriah said unto David, the ark and Israel and Judah abide in tents and my Lord Joab and the servants of my Lord are encamped in the open fields, shall I then go unto my house to eat and to drink and to lie with my wife as thou livest and as thy soul liveth? I will not do this thing. So David said to him, Stay here again tonight, and you will leave tomorrow.

And Uriah stayed in Jerusalem and the following morning David wrote a letter to Joab and sent it by the hand of Uriah and he wrote in the letter saying, Set Uriah in front of the hottest battle and retire from him that he may be smitten and die. And Joab did as the king directed him and the war went on, and many people of Joab's army died including Uriah.

Notice here the cruelty of King David who now has committed adultery and murder against Uriah's family. In Genesis 49:9, it states that, "Judah is a lion's whelp from the prey my son thou art gone up: he stooped down, he crouched as a lion, and as an old lion who shall rouse him up? Here you see the words spoken by Jacob his father being fulfilled" (Samuel 11:1-27).

Now when the time came for the baby to be delivered, David and Bathsheba had a baby boy and the king was so happy to have a son by Bathsheba because David loved her. But this act of evil displeased the Lord God of Israel and the Lord sent Prophet Nathan to David to inform him that he has despised the commandment of the Lord to do evil in his sight. Then the Lord was not happy with the things David had done. So God promised to punish David for his sins saying, "I will take your wives away and give them to other men of Israel, to lie with them in your eyes. And David said to Nathan the prophet, I have sinned against the Lord. And Nathan said unto David, the Lord also has put away the sin thou shall not die." But the child shall surely die. And David therefore besought God for the child and fasted all day and all night and the elders of Israel came to comfort him.

Now because David had accepted his faults through Prophet Nathan, God forgave him but not without punishment and David took Bathsheba for wife and later they had a son called Solomon who also became King of Israel because God loved him and eventually built the temple or the house of God to dwell in. David however was given more punishments by God for his family a destruction in the eyes of Israel. His son Amnon loved his sister Tamar and slept with her and defiled her and caused great sin in Israel. Then later Absalom David's son rose against him to battle in the war because Absalom wanted his father's throne. In the end, Absalom was killed as the war continued making King David lose credibility in the eyes of a great nation. Nevertheless, David was able to come out of all these adversities because he was the real anointed and chosen to be King and the high priest in Israel.

Let us now see how his legacy moves on and maybe we will have a better understanding of his kingship. Let us turn to the book of Ruth. We see Ruth who was a Moabite from the descendants of Lot coming to the picture in the rescue mission of the Jews people. When there was a famine in the land of Israel, there was a young woman whose name was Naomi. She had two sons and a husband. They went to the land of Moab and her two sons married Moabite women. Because Naomi's husband had died, they thought it would be a good idea to get themselves wives. Soon after that they both died and left two widowed young girls with their mother Naomi. In the process of time Naomi did not know what to do to keep them happy or to help them get husbands. So she asked them to return to their place maybe they can get married again. One of them whose name was Ruth said she would stay with her mother in law even if she goes back to Jerusalem. So Naomi decided to return to Jerusalem and Ruth came along with her. In the process of time Naomi and Ruth needed some food and Ruth being a young lady decided to go and work for it. Naomi had a relative named Boaz who was a very good businessman and had a corn field that many people in Israel would go and obtain some food through helping in the harvesting process. So Naomi had advised Ruth what she should do to meet Boaz. Ruth followed her mother in law's advice as she had promised her before that she would listen to her.

When Ruth met Boaz, they connected very well and finally they got married. See Ruth 4:12.

> And let the house be like the house Pharez whom Tamar bare into Judah of the seed which God shall give thee of this young woman. So Boaz took Ruth and Ruth became his wife. And they had a son who they named Obed who was the father of Jesse and Jesse the father of David. Now these are the generations of Pharez: Pharez begat Hezron and Hezron begat Ram and Ram begat Amminadab and Amminadab begat Nah'shon and Nah'shon begat Salmon who married Rahab the harlot (Joshua 2:1).

Salmon begat Boaz by Ruth and Boaz begat Obed and Obed begat Jesse and Jesse begat David and David begat Solomon and Solomon begat Jeroboam and at this point God changed and shifted the kingship temporarily to another tribe of Israel. Shortly after that, Israel was divided into Northern Kingdom and Southern Kingdom so there was Israel in the South and Judah in the North. Now this is the beginning of Israel's problems until the birth of our savior Jesus Christ. Remember Jesus when he was still on earth said that the kingdom divided against itself cannot stand." Israel after this went through the foreign powers oppression for several years. The Babylonian captivity, Persia, Greece, and Roman empires all ruled Jerusalem at one point or another. They never had organized government since the time of King Solomon to 1948 when Israel became a country and state and now the most powerful small country on the face of Earth. One thing still stands is that they have more enemies around them than any other country on earth. Very soon we will see all these enemies coming against them, but only to be defeated and destroyed by the lion of the tribe of Judah who's the greatest descendant. Jesus Christ will take the throne and his kingdom will have no end. So, in the last day Judah and Dan will remember the words of their father Jacob in Genesis 49.

ABOUT THE WRITER

I was born in 1950 in a small village called Ng'onyi in a district called Meru in Eastern Kenya in eastern Africa. Growing up in this part of the world was not an easy task because people depend on small skill farming peasant type where they raise few animals such as sheep, goats, cattle and livestock. I was the fourth of nine children but two left us in an early age to go and be with the Lord. I was about six or seven years old when I started helping my father with grazing sheep and goats and sometimes staying in the field with them all day. I did not get to go to school on time as the other kids of my age did in the community. I was feeling left out when I see other kids coming from school in the evening with their book bags on their backs and kicking tennis balls on their way home from school. I wanted very much to do the same thing but the opportunity was not there.

At the age of eight, I enrolled to a catechism class to become a Christian, as these courses were offered at nearby elementary school and the teacher was a neighbor and also he was a school teacher. One day I arrived early for my class and the school boys were playing soccer ball in the field. I joined them and kicked the ball a few times. Some boys went and reported me to the teacher that I kicked the ball and I was not enrolled in school. I got punished for that. It was a bad feeling.

The next thing I wanted to do was to enroll in school so I can kick the ball without being punished. I finished my catechism classes in April of 1959 and I was baptized. The following year in June of 1960, I enrolled in kindergarten and I and another friend of mine were the only two big boys in class. The others were five and six years old. So I was 11 years old when I started first grade. That did not bother me. I was doing well in class and I was kicking soccer ball without punishment.

As soon as I started 1st grade, I realized that I had bad vision and I was having a very hard time seeing the writing on the board. My teacher put me on the front desk but I was still having difficulties taking notes. Sometimes I would get up and walk close to the board and read the sentence and then return to my desk and write it down. My mother was very disturbed to find out about my condition because my older brother had lost his right foot caused by polio and he was using a walking cane or walking stick up to this day. Regardless of my condition, I continued to work hard. I had faith in God and I was doing well and had nothing to complain about. When the athletic season began years later in 1964, I tried to run 100 yards but the big boys were too good for me and I was losing to them all the time. The following year I tried the distance running and competed in six miles in local organized athletics or track and field.

I finished 3rd and won my first trophy and I was very excited. The next two years I ran the mile and did not do too well. In 1968 in the district championship I won the mile and went on to represent my province in the national championship and ran against the greatest man in the world, Kipchoge Keino. That year he won a gold medal in Mexico Olympics in 1968 in 1500 M. In the Olympic trials that year, I finished a distance 7th out of 12 finalists. At that point, I was encouraged by my efforts and started working even harder. In 1970 I enrolled at Nkubu secondary school and the competition was greater and hard work became more demanding. I did better in cross-country that year than track. Kipchoge Keino came to my school in 1971 and presented me with a pair of running shoes, Adidas, for winning a national cross-country meet and encouraged me to put more effort in my event.

By the time I was a senior in high school in 1973, I represented my province in national championship and won both 800 meters and 1500 meters setting Kenya high school records in both events. After high school, I joined Egoji Teacher's College where track and field was taken seriously. My roommate in high James Munyala was already at Egoji College. We both teamed up again as we did in high school and improved our times. In 1975 Kenya Colleges Championships, Munyala broke the 3,000 M Steeplechase record and I set 1,500 meters and 800 meters record respectively.

In April of 1975 Munyala got a track scholarship in the University of Texas at El Paso where he defended his 3,000 M Steeplechase title for three years only to lose to Henry Rono in the NCAA Championships in Eugene, Oregon in 1978. At that point, Rono had already broken 4 world records in distance running. Three months after Munyala left Egoji, I also received a track scholarship to attend Charleston Southern University in Charleston, South Carolina where I defended my Steeplechase state title 4 times in a row. The hard work and faith in God paid off but it was God who was leading the way and my job was to obey.

When I finished college, I returned to my native country Kenya and taught at Njiri's high school in Murang'a but the coup de' tat of 1982 changed my mind about staying in Kenya and so I returned to the United States.

Upon returning to the United States, I started working with the department of mental health and worked with special population group for several years. Then in 1998, my wife and I started a daycare facility to provide services to children in need. After 15 years, the county decided to change the way they do business and cut back on a lot of things. In May of 2013, we closed the daycare and my wife started a non-profit organization called Sister to Sister International providing services to children in various parts of Kenya and helping women on how to improve their lives by making a better living.

The last four years have been very hard for me because my eye doctor decided to operate on my eyes to insert lenses on them for my vision was deteriorating. After the operation, my vision got worse from 20/60 to 20/70. The Department of Motor Vehicles took away my driver's license which already had restrictions on it. So being borderline or half blind, there is not much I can do. One thing I know to do is trust God and He will direct your steps leading you to still waters and providing you with what you need. He led me to write this book and with poor vision he provided enough light for me to see. Let us praise him, honor him, and all glory be unto him. Amen!

Beloved,
Francis M. Ruchugo